MEN-AT-ARMS SERIE

EDITOR: MARTIN WINDR

The Alamo
and the War of
Texan Independence
1835-36

Text *by* PHILIP HAYTHORNTHWAITE

Colour plates by PAUL HANNON

OSPREY PUBLISHING LONDON

Published in 1986 by
Osprey Publishing Ltd
Member company of the George Philip Group
12–14 Long Acre, London WC2E 9LP
© Copyright 1986 Osprey Publishing Ltd
Reprinted 1986

British Library Cataloguing in Publication Data

Haythornthwaite, Philip J.
    The Alamo and the War of Texan Independence
    1835–36.—(Men-at-arms series; 173)
    1. Texas—History—Revolution, 1835–36
    I. Title   II. Series
    976.4'03   F390

    ISBN 0-85045-684-3

Filmset in Great Britain
Printed through Bookbuilders Ltd, Hong Kong

Artist's Note

Readers may care to note that the original paintings
from which the colour plates in this book were
prepared are available for private sale. All
reproduction copyright whatsoever is retained by the
publisher. All enquiries should be addressed to:
    Paul Hannon
    90 Station Road
    Kings Langley
    Herts WD4 8LB
The publishers regret that they can enter into no
correspondence upon this matter.

Acknowledgements

Among the many individuals and institutions who
provided valuable assistance, the following deserve
special mention: Martha Utterback and Nina L.
Nixon of the staff of the Daughters of the Republic of
Texas at the Alamo; Thomas E. DeVoe for his help,
especially for allowing use of material in his
possession; H. V. Wilkinson for supplying copies of
early sources; and especial thanks to Kevin R. Young
of Presidio La Bahia, whose unfailing help was of the
greatest possible value. To these and all others who
assisted, the author's gratitude; but any errors,
omissions or expressions of opinion are his
responsibility alone.   PJH

Author's Note

Though contemporary spellings have been used
throughout the text, some concessions have been
made to modern usage: e.g. in the name 'San
Antonio', which is an abbreviation for 'San Antonio
de Bexar', which was often termed simply 'Bexar' in
the 1830s. At this period the inhabitants of Texas
were commonly styled 'Texians', which is the term
employed here.

The Alamo and Texan Independence 1835-36

Historical Background

'It does not appear to me possible that there can be a land more lovely,' wrote an early visitor to Texas; and Mary Austin Holley's 1836 guidebook claimed: 'One feels that Omnipotence has here consecrated in the bosom of Nature and under Heaven's wide canopy, a glorious temple in which to receive praise and adoration of the grateful beholder.' A bountiful paradise was one side of Texas's nature; the other was characterised by extremes of climate, and marauding Indians.

In 1727 a Spanish colony to the north of Mexico was formed into the province of Tejas or Texas (named from the local Indians), where settlements had been thrust into the wilderness since 1690. Beset by hostiles and by a lack of real zeal to open up the area, settlements were restricted to small enclaves around the ecclesiastical, military and civil bases (missions, *presidios* and *pueblos* respectively). By 1821 it was estimated that (excluding Indians) the population of Texas numbered only some 4,000, mostly around the *presidios* of San Antonio de Bexar and La Bahía. The emptiness of the land could not fail to attract settlers from the United States, whose boundaries lay along the Sabine and Red Rivers; and US expansionism following the Louisiana Purchase made it inevitable that Americans would become entangled in Mexican affairs. In 1812–13 a force of Mexican rebels and American adventurers captured San Antonio and La Bahía, but were slaughtered by a Spanish army at the Medina River; among the Spanish officers present was one Lt. Antonio López de Santa Anna Pérez de Lebrón, who figures largely in the story which follows.

In the war which won Mexico her independence from Spain in 1821, Santa Anna at first supported Spain, then changed sides when it became obvious that the future lay with independence. Almost immediately, Mexico was split by internal conflict between the conservative centralists, who wanted a strong central government, and the liberal federalists, who favoured a loose confederation of semi-autonomous provinces. The confusion was resolved temporarily in May 1822 when Gen. Iturbide, instigator of the revolt against Spain, proclaimed himself Emperor Agustín I; but, after initially supporting him, Santa Anna soon undermined the Emperor, and was largely responsible for a revolt which ousted Iturbide and proclaimed a federalist republic. A Congress was called, and produced the Constitution of 1824; modelled upon that of the United States, this theoretically guaranteed justice for every citizen and a chance of improving the generally wretched lot of the majority.

Antonio López de Santa Anna, President of Mexico and commander-in-chief of the Army of Operations in Texas. (Contemporary engraving)

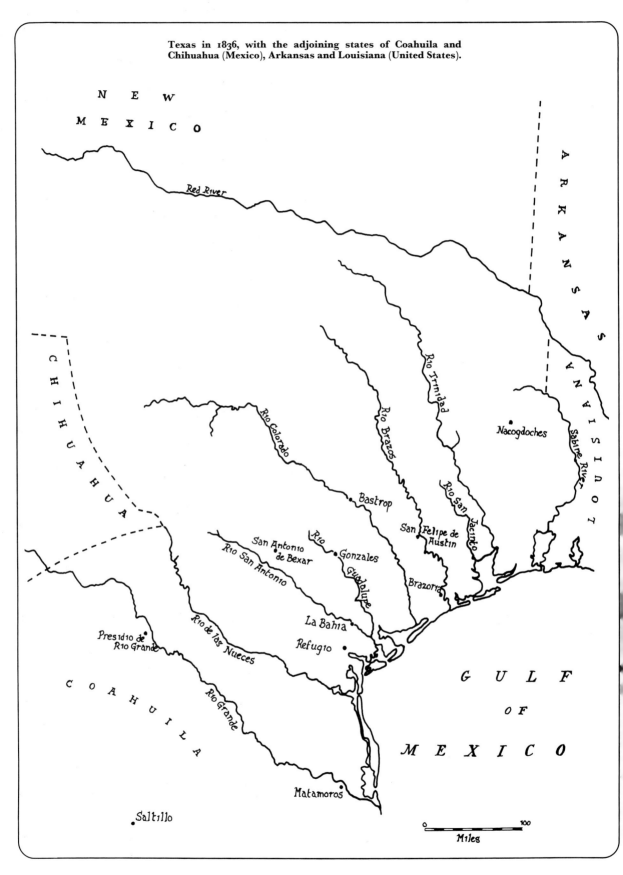

Texts in 1836, with the adjoining states of Coahuila and Chihuahua (Mexico), Arkansas and Louisiana (United States).

N E W
M E X I C O

Red River

A R K A N S A S

L O U I S I A N A

C H I H U A H U A

Rio Colorado

Rio Brazos

Rio Trinidad

Rio San Jacinto

Sabine River

Nacogdoches

Bastrop

San Felipe de Austin

Rio
San Antonio
de Bexar

Rio San Antonio

Gonzales

Guadalupe

Brazoria

La Bahia

Presidio de
Rio Grande

Rio de las Nueces

Refugio

C O A H U I L A

Rio Grande

G U L F

O F

M E X I C O

Matamoros

Saltillo

0 100
Miles

The last months of Spanish rule had seen a desperate experiment in Texas: in an attempt to prevent illegal settlement, responsible Americans were awarded large land grants, the settlers being required to accept Mexican citizenship and Roman Catholicism. The first of the American contractors or *empresarios* was the Missourian Moses Austin, whose son Stephen succeeded to his grants in 1821. The grants were renegotiated with Congress, and in April 1823 Texas was opened officially to American settlement; over the next 12 years almost 28,000 Americans took advantage of the opportunity. Not unnaturally, they attempted to establish American standards of liberty in their new communities, their criticisms of the Mexican system of justice and organisation causing the Mexicans to regard them as uncouth ingrates; repressive measures followed, which drove the two communities wider apart.

During this period Santa Anna had grown ever more powerful. A corrupt and ruthless politician, thief, compulsive gambler, opium addict and liar, he was known to his countrymen as *Don Demonio* ('Sir Devil')—until, in August 1829, he defeated a half-hearted Spanish attempt to reconquer Mexico at the battle of Tampico: thereafter he became the self-styled 'Napoleon of the West'. Though a megalomaniac (who declared, 'Were I made God, I should wish to be something more'), he possessed military skill and a charismatic presence. By means of his Tampico reputation, several double-crosses and a revolution, he had himself elected liberal president in 1833; within a year he changed his stance, dismissed Congress, and set about destroying federalism.

Fears that Texas (though administratively connected with the province of Coahuila) was becoming too Americanised resulted in a series of measures to re-establish central authority, including the increase of military garrisons, and a ban on further American immigration from April 1830. Ironically, the leaders of the American colonists saw Santa Anna, ostensibly a liberal, as their saviour; but though the ban failed to stop immigration, it strengthened the militant faction among the Americans and undermined Austin's assertions of Mexican goodwill. After a skirmish between Mexicans and colonists at Velasco in June 1832, the Americans—their preferred name was 'Texians'—held a convention at San Felipe to prepare a formal

Capture of San Antonio by the Texians, December 1835. As the appearance of the town and the costume of the combatants would not be familiar to the majority of artists, this contemporary print shows the troops wearing conventional military uniform (with shakos), while the architectural details are obscured by smoke!

proposal for autonomy, including increased representation in Congress and separation from Coahuila. When Santa Anna emerged victorious from the brief civil war in Mexico, a second convention was called in April 1833 to press the Texians' case; Austin remained their leader, despite a growing radical element which sought even greater freedom.

A new character entered the scene in December 1832 when Sam Houston crossed the Red River into Texas. Descended from a Scottish emigrant to Virginia, the 39-year-old Houston could already boast a colourful career: ex-General of Militia, ex-Governor of Tennessee, and a confidant of President Jackson, he had been wounded twice in the War of 1812, adopted by the Cherokees, had practised as a lawyer, had achieved a reputation for courage in campaigning against the Creeks, and had been ruined by a disastrous marriage—after which he had returned to the Cherokees and won his Indian name, 'Big Drunk'. Rehabilitated by a crusade to expose dishonest Indian agents, Houston declared in the Congress, pointing to the Stars and Stripes: 'So long as that flag shall bear aloft its glittering stars, so long shall the rights of American citizens be preserved safe.' This was no bad motto for the Texians, and Houston became the darling of the radicals; he even suggested to Jackson that the United States might consider 'acquiring' Texas, given that nineteen-twentieths of the population were dissatisfied with a Mexican government which must remain despotic for the foreseeable future.

In 1833 Austin was flung into gaol for expressing pro-independence sentiments, though he continued to urge his compatriots to remain passive. Santa Anna's increasing despotism caused federalist rebellions in eight states; in April 1835 he crushed a revolt in Zacatecas, a state bordering Coahuila, and sent his brother-in-law Gen. Martín Perfecto de Cós to extinguish resistance in Coahuila itself. In June despatches fell into the hands of the Texians at San Felipe announcing the suspension of civil government, and that Santa Anna was planning to discipline the Americans personally. Popular sentiment fell in behind the Texian 'war party'; but though the garrison of the Mexican customs post at Anahuac was ejected by a fiery young South Carolinan lawyer, William Barret Travis, passive councils prevailed; and the peace party re-affirmed that the Texians wished only for a good understanding with the Mexican government. As Cós began to move his troops into Texas, Austin arrived back from prison—with an altered perspective. Declaring Santa Anna a 'base, unprincipled bloody monster', he stated: 'War is our only recourse. No halfway measures, but war in full.' Once awakened, the 'Spirit of '76' galvanised the colonists—however much they yearned for peace—into open rebellion.

A Mexican detachment was sent from San Antonio to repossess a useless old cannon loaned to the citizens of Gonzales in 1831 to frighten Indians, which served only to 'make a noise whenever the people got into a merry frolic', but which now became a symbol of independence. Beneath a banner reading 'Come and Take It', the Texians assembled, saying that the cannon belonged to the Federal Republic, not the central government. Just south of Gonzales, on 2 October 1835, the war began with a ragged fusillade from the Texians which killed one Mexican and scattered the remainder.

Santa Anna's march to Texas, showing the dates of his arrival at the various points on his route. Leaving Mexico City on 28 November 1835, he delayed at San Luis Potosí in December to organise the army, and delayed a further three weeks at Saltillo. He entered Texas on 16 February 1836.

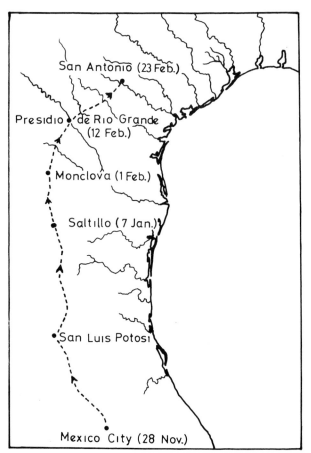

The War of Texan Independence

Cós had 1,400 men in San Antonio; many were of poor quality, as the worst had been sent to Texas—often criminals in what were virtual penal regiments; the later reinforcements were of higher calibre. Around 500 Texians gathered at Gonzales, resembling an armed mob more than an army. Though some had military experience, the majority were untrained farmers; but they included enough frontiersmen with the traditional 'long rifles' to make them a formidable enemy in unconventional warfare. Stephen Austin was elected commander, though he was unwell, unfitted for the job, and unable to keep any order in a force which came and went as it pleased. Houston accepted a local command, then set off to the Texian convention at San Felipe.

The 'army', now around 300 strong, decided to attack San Antonio, and Austin could only accede to the wish of the majority. On 27 October a small Texian force routed a larger Mexican one at

Concepción mission, two miles south of San Antonio; the Texians had one man killed, while the Mexicans lost 67 dead and as many wounded to the Texian sharpshooting. The Texians were led by James Bowie, a charismatic adventurer famous for his business acumen in obtaining vast tracts of Texas, and even more so for a reputation as a duellist which he had literally carved out with his famous knife. An ardent patriot, he had been heartbroken by the death of his wife and family in 1833, since when alcohol had become his solace. His deputy at Concepción was James Walker Fannin, a Georgian who had failed to graduate from West Point, but who showed organisational talent if no great military genius. Despite their success, however, the Texians were in no position to assault Cós' entrenched position, and so settled down for a siege.

The Texian convention opened at San Felipe on 3 November: 'plenty of recklessness and selfishness', wrote Anson Jones; 'I was introduced to Bowie—he was dead drunk; to Houston—his appearance was anything but decent or respectable, and very much like that of a broken-down sot and debauchee.' This body had to decide upon a declaration of independence or an affirmation of loyalty to the 1824 Constitution. Houston, surprisingly, argued for the latter course—to oppose Santa Anna as loyal Mexican citizens should. This was decided upon, with an added offer to help any other Mexican state which took up arms 'against military despotism'. Austin was sent to the United States to appeal for help; and command of the army devolved upon an old Indian-fighter, Edward Burleson.

Among the American Texans opposition to Santa Anna was virtually solid, and appeals to the USA varied from the rational to the histrionic. Houston declared that 'War in defence of our rights, our oaths, and our constitution is inevitable . . . If volunteers from the United States will join their brethren in this section, they will receive liberal bounties of land . . . Let each man come with a good rifle and one hundred rounds of ammunition—and . . . come soon. Our war cry is "LIBERTY OR DEATH!!"' Similar appeals repeated the twin attractions of aid to kindred in distress, and land-grants for all volunteers: '. . . we are but one people. Our fathers, side by side, fought the revolution . . . our interest is one . . . WE HAVE

Sam Houston: an engraving just post-dating San Jacinto (from *South America and Mexico, with a complete View of Texas*, J. M. Niles, 1838)

THE FINEST COUNTRY ON THE FACE OF THE GLOBE. WE INVITE YOU TO ENJOY IT WITH US . . . We will secure . . . our constitutional rights and privileges, or we shall leave Texas a howling wilderness!' . . . 'MARCH!! Victory awaits you; the Genius of Liberty has unfurled her banners and will crown her children with imperishable laurels . . . let the tyrant fall in a war of extermination . . .'

The appeal was ·irresistible. Throughout the United States, but especially the South, volunteer companies were organised, and men and munitions began to flood into Texas. Not all the USA sided with the Texians, however. The *Baltimore Gazette*, for example, published a violent argument for non-interference ('There is not the slightest shadow of right on the side of the Texonians'); but most agreed with the *Troy Daily Whig*—that once independence had been declared, Texas was no longer part of Mexico; and just as the infant United States had been aided by France and Spain, 'shall we fail in conceding that support to Texas which we desired and required when placed in similar circumstances?'

Such support, however, was entirely 'private': at least officially, the United States remained strictly neutral, even though Gen. Gaines, US commander on the border and under orders to protect US neutrality, seems to have had a strong inclination to enter the war on the Texian side. Ordered to prevent Indian raids from the US into unprotected parts of Texas, he believed it his duty to anticipate the 'lawless movements' of the 'Mexicans, or their red allies ... by crossing our supposed or imaginary national boundary, and meeting the savage marauders wherever to be found'! In the event, Texian victory obviated the need for US intervention; but Gaines' dispatch of dragoons and the 7th Infantry to Nacogdoches in July 1836 (they were only withdrawn in December, despite being in a 'foreign' state) seems evidence of his determination to exert what pressure he could.

However, as the pro-independence faction won ground in Texas, many Texians of Mexican descent (or *Tejanos*) became alarmed at the attitude of the Americans, as most of the volunteers did not appreciate the ideals of the 1824 Constitution. Consequently, while many *Tejanos* fought against Santa Anna, others sided with him; like Don Carlos de la Garza, one of La Bahía's leading citizens, who

Plan of the Alamo as it appeared in the mid-1760s. The complex included a two-storey *convento* (friary) with patios and workshops, a granary, a fortified tower at the main gate, and a plaza surrounded by the dwellings of the mission Indians built on the inside of the perimeter wall; in 1762 some 275 people lived in the mission. The church was never completed and the sacristy seems to have been the centre for religious services. The whole is typical of a religious and defensive foundation on the frontier, the church and *convento* representing the spiritual and administrative part of the mission, and the Indian apartments and workshops the secular aspects.

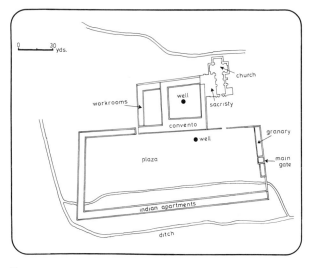

organised for Santa Anna a company styled the 'Victorian Guards'.

San Antonio and its consequences

The besiegers of San Antonio were reinforced by volunteers from the USA, some joining individually and others in organised units, like the two (separate) companies of New Orleans Greys. The local Texian troops exhibited the concept of democracy gone mad; they totally lacked discipline, and all decisions depended upon a vote amongst the officers. As winter approached and volunteers began to drift home, a council of field officers overruled Burleson and decided to withdraw. The volunteers from the United States were more determined: as Capt. Cooke of the New Orleans Greys said, they had not come to Texas simply to 'lie three or four months in the colonies'. San Antonio, however, was strongly entrenched, and garrisoned by one regular battalion (Morelos) and at least five presidial companies; one of their strongpoints was the fortified mission known as the Alamo (either after the cottonwood (*álamo*) trees that grew nearby, or because it had served as a barracks for the company from Alamo de Parras in Mexico).

The problem was resolved by 'Colonel' Ben Milam, a Kentucky adventurer who had fought for Mexican independence, and recently escaped from the gaol where he had languished for his republican sympathies since Iturbide's time. Declaring, 'Boys, who will come with old Ben Milam into San Antonio?', he led the Texians (New Orleans Greys in the van) into the town. Four days of house-to-house fighting, in which Milam was killed by a sharpshooter, ended on 9 December when Cós opened negotiations for surrender. Burleson accepted, gave the Mexicans enough weapons to protect themselves against Indians, and sent them home on the condition that they would not again fight against the 1824 Constitution. After their brilliant victory (300 defeating 1,400 Mexicans in a defended position), most Texians believed the war over and went home. Houston, realising that it had only just begun, went unheeded as he appealed, 'Let the brave rally to the standard.'

Of the Texians who remained under arms, many were lured into a mad scheme for the invasion of Mexico and the capture of Matamoros, at the

Alamo Church + Plaza

mouth of the Rio Grande, where they believed an alliance with Mexican liberals could overturn Santa Anna; the potential loot of Matamoros was an added appeal, and thus Col. James C. Neill was left with but 104 men to hold the improvised fortress of the Alamo.

The crumbling walls of the old mission had probably been strengthened by the Mexicans in 1835, but were now put into as good a state of defence as possible by Green Jameson, a Kentucky lawyer turned military engineer. The derelict mission church had strong walls, if no roof. There was a two-storey stone building called the 'Long Barracks', and a single-storey 'Low Barracks' pierced by the main gate, itself protected by an earthwork 'lunette'. More than 20 Mexican cannon had been abandoned in the Alamo, which were re-mounted and placed upon earthwork ramparts inside the 12-foot-high wall which surrounded the Alamo compound, a rough rectangle enclosing about three acres. Its perimeter stretched to about a

The earliest photograph of the Alamo, as it appeared c.1852–53. The Long Barracks (repaired and re-roofed by the US Army by 1847) are at the left; the chapel was re-roofed and the facade built up to include the 'hump' or parapet in about 1850. This latter feature, which has given the Alamo its unique silhouette, was neither part of the original design nor present in 1836. The cannon in the right foreground was one of those excavated in 1852, probably one of those smashed and buried by the Mexicans after the battle. (Library, Daughters of the Republic of Texas at the Alamo)

quarter of a mile, requiring a huge garrison to defend it adequately. The weakest section was a 75-foot gap in the wall between the Low Barracks and the church, closed by a palisaded earthwork. As an improvised fortress it had more weaknesses than strengths.

Houston, attempting to organise the state's 'regular' army, was appalled by the prospect of the Matamoros expedition; but the legislative council in San Felipe approved, and nominated James Fannin to command. Governor Henry Smith, nominal head of the state of Texas, railed at the council for this decision, and dismissed it until 1

9

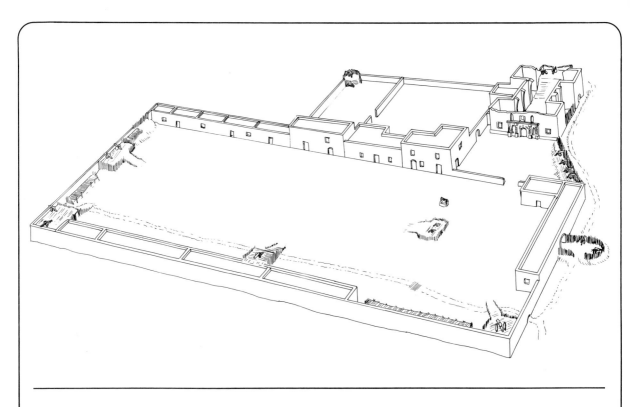

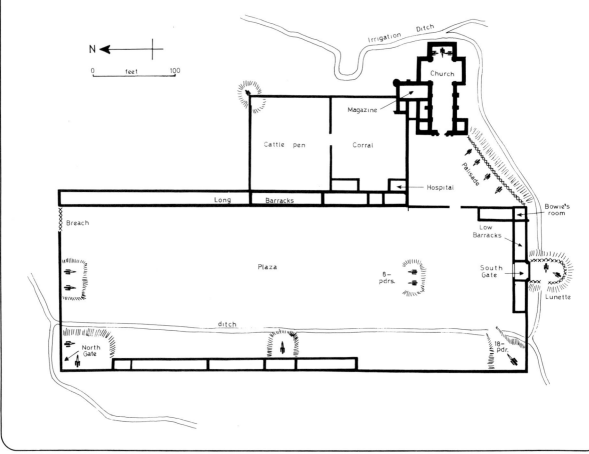

Irrigation Ditch

Church

Magazine

Cattle pen

Corral

Hospital

Palisade

Long   Barracks

Breach

Bowie's room

Low Barracks

Plaza

8- pdrs.

South Gate

Lunette

ditch

North Gate

18- pdr.

N

0   feet   100

March, when a new body would meet at Washington-on-the-Brazos; the council, in turn, dismissed Smith, calling him 'vulgar and depraved'. Both government and army were in chaos; Neill's Alamo garrison was starving and deserting ('If there has ever been a dollar here I have no knowledge of it'), and around La Bahía Fannin's men were roaming about working themselves up to invade Mexico. Since Fannin acknowledged no authority but that of the legislative council, Houston (nominal commander of the army) had no control over them, but he went among the men, using his personality to convince them that every man would be required to defend Texas from the coming storm. Enough Texians at La Bahía were sufficiently impressed to decide to wait and think again, only 70 men going with Col. Frank Johnson and Dr James Grant to Matamoros—and annihilation . . .

As Houston realised, Santa Anna had no intention of relinquishing his grip on Texas, and was preparing an army to crush the opposition. Though mediocre by the standards of the European armies upon which he modelled it, Santa Anna's force contained a core of experienced, if somewhat venal, officers and some well-disciplined troops. Modelled upon Napoleonic lines, the Mexican army assembled by Santa Anna included both 'regulars' and 'active militia', the latter virtually as competent as the former. His administration might be wretched and totally corrupt, and his supply system ineffective; but Santa Anna spent vast sums of borrowed money on perfecting his Army of Operations in Texas, which probably stood at about 6,000 men, plus reinforcements which swelled the Mexican presence in Texas to about 7,500 by mid-April. For all its imperfections, it was far more formidable than the wretched opposition encountered by the Texians thus far.

Houston planned to concentrate the Texians and avoid a pitched battle, wearing down the Mexicans at long range and extending Santa Anna's supply lines until the right moment to strike. Accordingly, he sent Bowie with 30 volunteers to the Alamo, with orders to withdraw after destroying the fort; Neill's situation had by now deteriorated so far that he reported having only 80 men left, unpaid, 'almost naked' and 'in a torpid, defenceless situation'. But despite Houston's faith in Bowie, no evacuation occurred: Neill had no means of transporting his cannon. Bowie found the men ready to defend the Alamo when Santa Anna should arrive—as arrive he must, San Antonio being on his obvious invasion route along the old Spanish road, *El Camino Real*. Using his contacts in the Mexican community to procure supplies for the Alamo, Bowie organised a resolution demanding reinforcements: 'We cannot be driven from the post of honor.' He added, in a letter to Governor Smith, that San Antonio was the vital 'picquet guard' to Texas, the maintenance of which was imperative; 'Colonel Neill and myself have come to the solemn resolution that we will rather die in these ditches than give it up to the enemy.' Houston's plans were confounded; with no men under his command, with first Fannin and now Bowie and Neill refusing to obey him, he attempted to resign in disgust, but was given leave by Governor Smith until 1 March. He used the opportunity to travel among the Cherokees to ensure that they, at least, would remain at peace while the Texians were engaged with Santa Anna.

Santa Anna's advance

After a grand review of his Army of Operations, on 1 February 1836 Santa Anna led his army (one cavalry and two infantry brigades, artillery, and the crack engineer corps of *Zapadores*) from Saltillo towards the Rio Grande to join Gen. Joaquin Sesma's men already there, while a smaller force under Gen. José Urrea headed for Matamoros. The march towards Texas became a nightmare as the Mexican army shuffled and starved its way through

Opposite, above: **Likely appearance of the Alamo during the siege. It is probable that palisade and earthwork ramparts were constructed along the outer wall where no flat roof was available as a fire-step, since similar constructions were raised as artillery platforms. Unlike some modern reconstructions, the cattle pen is shown here as bounded by a wall instead of a palisade, with a palisaded gun position raised at the north-east corner—plans of the late 1840s clearly show the footings of a wall. The battery of two 8-pdrs. in the plaza acted as a redoubt to cover the south gate, should it be forced; and the irrigation ditch which ran parallel to the west wall inside the plaza could also be used as a defensive trench. Travis was killed near to the battery of two 8-pdrs. at the centre of the north wall.**

Opposite, below: **Plan of the defences of the Alamo as they probably appeared during the siege, taken in part from plans of the surviving structures executed in the late 1840s, at which time part of the Long Barracks, Low Barracks and buildings on the east wall were still in existence, though the perimeter walls had been demolished. The breach in the north wall was closed by a palisade. The north gate was a postern situated below the rampart.**

the dust and later the snow of the hills of Coahuila, leaving a trail of broken transport, corpses and dead pack animals. Reduced to half rations, the soldiers ate mesquite nuts and other vegetation; dysentery followed, and felled even more. 'Their sufferings only spur them to greater efforts' was the official comment.

Reinforcements arrived at the Alamo: on 3 February, William B. Travis, the young lawyer who believed himself marked for greatness, now a lieutenant-colonel of Texian cavalry, with 30 men; and on 8 February, the most famous frontiersman of his day, 'Colonel' David Crockett and his small Tennessee Company of Mounted Volunteers. Bear-hunter, Indian-fighter, ex-Congressman, *raconteur par excellence*, and a living legend, 'Davy' Crockett had come to Texas 'to aid you all that I can in your noble cause'. By 10 February the Alamo garrison numbered 142, a mixture of colonists and new arrivals (including part of the New Orleans Greys who had chosen not to go to Matamoros; the latter joined either the Mobile Grays, or changed their title to the San Antonio Grays[1]). Their origins were as diverse as their occupations, embracing all corners of the United States as well as England, Scotland, Ireland, France—and Mexico.

Perhaps overawed by the three powerful leaders now in the garrison, Neill left the Alamo on 20 days' leave, turning the command over to Travis, the senior regular officer—though inferior to Bowie in

[1]Both spellings were current—'greys', 'grays'.

Siege of the Alamo: siting of the Mexican batteries, numbered 1 to 6. Battery 5 was sited by the old powder house on the Gonzales road; battery 6 was that established within 250 yards of the Alamo on 4 March, and later even closer. 'La Villita' was the shanty town south and east of San Antonio; the cross identifies San Fernando Church in the centre of the town.

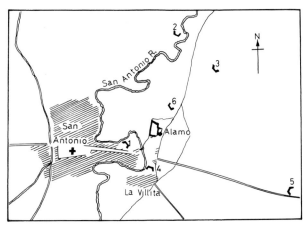

the eyes of the volunteers. Bowie was desperately ill, however, and usually making a drunken nuisance of himself in San Antonio. A temporary peace was established between the leaders on 14 February when Travis and Bowie agreed to share command. Two days later Santa Anna crossed the Rio Grande, having united his forces with those of Gen. Sesma at Presidio de Rio Grande. Preparations continued at the Alamo; the defences were strengthened and munitions gathered, horseshoes were chopped into grapeshot, a hospital was established, and the wives and children of some of the defenders were sheltered in the mission. Travis began a series of pleas for assistance, directed principally to Fannin, who was now firmly ensconced in La Bahía, rechristened 'Fort Defiance'.

The Siege of the Alamo

A month before he was expected, Santa Anna arrived in San Antonio on 23 February. Helter-skelter, the garrison and its dependants—about 150 men and 25 non-combatants—retired into the Alamo. Travis despatched another appeal to Fannin, and one to the nearest town which might be able to send reinforcements, Gonzales, about 70 miles east. Santa Anna began his investment of the Alamo, hoisting on the church belfry of San Antonio a red banner, the symbol of no quarter. By way of reply Travis fired a shot from the Alamo's heaviest cannon, an 18-pdr. mounted at the south-east corner.

On 24 February the Mexican bombardment opened as their encirclement drew tighter around the Alamo; and Travis wrote his most famous message, in typically theatrical style: '. . . our flag still waves proudly from the walls—*I shall never surrender or retreat.* Then, I call on you in the name of Liberty, of patriotism & everything dear to the American character, to come to our aid . . . If this call is neglected, I am determined to sustain myself as long as possible & die like a soldier who never forgets what is due to his honor & that of his country—*Victory or Death.*' Early that morning, Travis assumed sole command, as Bowie's health had finally collapsed and he had taken to his bed.

The bombardment continued on 25 February, and a fire-fight developed between Mexicans scattering through peasant shacks to the south of the

Alamo and Crockett's Tennesseeans. The Tennessee company had been assigned the most vulnerable section of the defences, the stockade on the south face; they were supported by artillery in the lunette and the chapel, which was directed by the Alamo's two artillery officers, Capts. Almeron Dickinson (a Gonzales blacksmith, whose wife and baby were in the compound) and William Carey from Baltimore. A lightning raid burned the shacks which could have sheltered Mexican sharpshooters; the garrison suffered no casualties. Another appeal from Travis was carried out by Capt. Juan Seguin, a prominent San Antonio *Tejano* whose company was in the garrison: 'It will be impossible for us to keep them out much longer. If they overpower us, we fall a sacrifice at the shrine of our country, and we hope posterity will do our memory justice. Give me help, oh my Country!'

On 26 February Fannin stirred himself to march to Travis's relief; but when a supply-waggon broke down after a few hundred yards, he postponed the advance for a day; and on the 27th he decided to return to Fort Defiance. But Travis's earlier message to Gonzales *had* been heeded, by the 25-strong Gonzales Ranging Company of Mounted Volunteers. Knowing the critical situation of the Alamo, they freely elected to join Travis—even Isaac Millsaps, who had a blind wife and seven children to support. Led by Lt. George Kimball, a New York hatter, and including the town sheriff and an English shoemaker, the tiny unit left all that was dear to them and slipped quietly into the Alamo just after midnight on the 29th. History contains few nobler actions than their decision to join Travis in his perilous position.

As Santa Anna's strength grew, the noose pulled tighter. Flagging morale in the Alamo was revived by Davy Crockett's fiddle, playing duets—or duels!—with the bagpipes of John McGregor, a Scot from Nacogdoches. Though too late to help the Alamo, Travis's appeals were beginning to galvanise Texas into action. On 2 March the reconvened convention at Washington-on-the-Brazos declared Texas an independent state; ironically, the Alamo garrison never realised that they were fighting officially for the Republic of Texas. Fannin decided to march again, to join up with volunteers who were assembling under Seguin and to march together to relieve the Alamo—but

once again, he postponed his advance. Another courier left the Alamo on the night of 3 March carrying further appeals from Travis, who was now resigned: 'The victory will cost the enemy so dear, that it will be worse for him than defeat.' Other notes were carried by the courier, most poignant being Isaac Millsaps' letter to his blind wife and 'My dear dear ones': describing the fortress 'that has most fell down' and the fact that the defenders had suffered no casualties, he said that he had watched the Mexicans drilling, 'marching up and down with such order', and that if only Fannin would come 'there would be a good fight'. Travis, he said, 'stays on the wall some but mostly in his room I hope help comes soon cause we cant fight them all'. Travis was going to speak to the garrison that evening, and 'if we fail here get to the river with the children all Texas will be before the enemy . . . There is no discontent in our boys some are tired from loss of sleep and rest. The Mexicans are shooting every few

Reconstruction of a Mexican map of the Alamo, drawn prior to the assault. While not in proportion, it does show the habitable buildings (shaded) including an L-shaped block at the north-east corner, and earthen gun platforms and ramps. The positions of the other batteries are shown by cannon symbols. Trenches appear around the north-east corner, along the south wall and around the lunette, a circular trench at the north-east corner of the corral, and inside the north wall of the corral. The building marked 'CP' here was identified by the Mexicans as the artillery command post; it was next to the 18-pdr. mounted at the south-west corner.

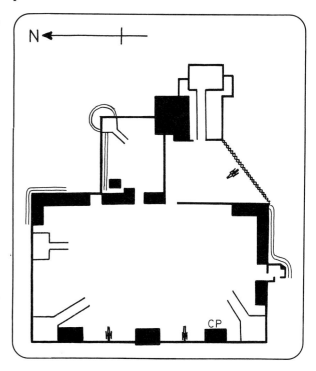

The Alamo chapel, as it appears today. (The Alamo)

The facade of the Alamo chapel is a familiar symbol which appears in most non-contemporary depictions of the battle. Its conventional appearance, however, is that of the reconstructed facade, very different from its appearance in 1836. The upper work, including the upper windows, did not exist in 1836. These front elevations show (*above*) the familiar, modern appearance, as compared to (*below*) the facade as it existed in 1836.

minutes . . . kiss the dear children for me and believe as I do that all will be well & God protect us.'

On Friday morning, 4 March, a Mexican battery had pushed within 250 yards to the north of the Alamo; Travis's last message, a despairing appeal to Fannin probably sent on the night of 5 March, noted that 'every shot goes through, as the walls are weak'. A sense of doom lay over the garrison; Crockett remarked that 'I think we had better march out and die in the open air. I don't like to be hemmed up', and a few Mexican defenders slipped away to rejoin their families in the town. Late on 5 March (though it could have been the 3rd, as Millsaps suggests) Travis called the garrison together and made a speech. The content is uncertain, but the crux was that he was staying in the Alamo to kill as many Mexicans as possible when the assault came. Whether he drew a line in the dust with his sabre, over which all who wished to remain were to step, is equally uncertain; tradition states that Bowie called for his cot to be carried over the line, and was seconded by Crockett. Apparently only one man chose to leave—one of Bowie's volunteers, a French veteran of the Napoleonic Wars named Louis Rose, who appears to have made good his escape. Whether Travis drew a line or when he spoke to the garrison is not significant; all that matters is the fact that they were resolved to hold to the last man.

Santa Anna had been reinforced by Gaona's Brigade on 3 March, and now had over 2,000 men at his disposal for the assault; the estimate that he used 4,000 is an exaggeration. Apparently about 1,800 were actually employed, in four columns of attack plus a reserve. The first column would strike the north-west corner; commanded by Cós, it comprised the Aldama Bn. and three companies of the San Luis. At the north-east, Col. Fransisco Duque and Gen. Castrillon commanded the Toluca Bn. and the balance of the San Luis. On the east, Col. Jose Maria Romero commanded the Matamoros and Jiménez fusilier companies; at the south was Col. Juan Morales with the light companies of the Matamoros, Jiménez and San Luis. Santa Anna commanded the reserve: the *Zapadores* battalion and the grenadier companies of the battalions Matamoros, Jiménez, Aldama, Toluca and San Luis. Apparently the standard European practice was followed of attacking in column with the light troops on either flank as a screen. All columns carried scaling ladders and crowbars.

The Final Assault

At 5 am on 6 March a bugle-call sounded from the Mexican lines, and a shout of 'Viva Santa Anna!' Travis's adjutant and official second-in-command, the Virginian Capt. John J. Baugh, was on the walls as duty officer; he ran towards the barracks shouting, 'Colonel Travis! The Mexicans are coming!' Grabbing his shotgun, Travis ran to the north wall, crying time and again 'Hurrah, my boys!' and, to some of Seguin's company, '*No rendirse, muchachos!*' The Alamo cannon fired a few shots—Duque was killed, and one volley swept away half the Toluca Battalion's chasseur company—but the attackers soon reached the walls where the cannon could not be depressed sufficiently. The Texians now relied upon their rifles, some men having four or five loaded and stacked beside them. Scaling-ladders were raised; Travis, leaning over the wall, was hit in the head and rolled down the rampart, dying. Texian fire forced all but Morales's column to congregate at the north, where they milled for some time; the

'Colonel' David Crockett: frontiersman, sometime politician, commander of the 'Tennessee Company of Mounted Volunteers', and arguably the most famous of the Alamo's defenders. (Contemporary engraving)

Mexican bands struck up the *Degüello*, the Spanish tune of 'no quarter', but it was probably the committing of the reserve which gave the Mexicans the impetus to scale the repaired breach in the north wall (though the Mexican Col. de la Peña claimed that the reserve was not needed).

As the north wall was scaled, the northern postern was forced by Cós's men, who had escaladed the north-west corner. The Mexicans flooded into the Alamo compound, just as Morales scaled the south-west angle, where the 18-pdr. was overrun. Baugh ordered the abandonment of the walls and withdrawal to the Long Barracks, where last-ditch positions had been prepared; but with Mexican sharpshooters in the water-course running the length of the compound, the Texians suffered severely. A few tried to break out, but were cut down by the waiting cavalry. The Texian cannon were now swung around by the Mexicans and used to blast the Long Barracks. Crockett's Tennesseeans were overrun before they could reach it, and the

James Bowie: a portrait showing a very elaborately hilted knife. (Daughters of the Republic of Texas)

flag of the New Orleans Greys was torn down from its position over the barracks. Morales's men burst into the Low Barracks, where Bowie lay mortally ill, and they tossed his body on their bayonets like a bale of straw. The 18-pdr. was swung around to blow in the doors of the church, where Dickinson still held out with James Bonham, the South Carolinan officer who had returned to die at the Alamo after carrying a fruitless appeal to Fannin. Charging into the church, the Mexicans slaughtered everyone who moved, including the two young sons of the English gunner Antony Wolfe. The Irish volunteer Robert Evans attempted to blow up the powder stored in the church, but was shot down. By 6.30 am the Alamo lay silent.

The non-combatants—Mrs Dickinson and her child, Bowie's sisters-in-law, Travis's slave and a few others—were protected by the courteous Mexican officers; not so the six Texians who surrendered, who were hacked to death upon Santa Anna's

orders. It is difficult to assess the casualties of the battle; 182 out of 183 defenders died (the single survivor, one Brigido Guerrero, convinced the Mexicans that he had been a prisoner of the Texians), while Santa Anna's losses were probably around 600. The story that up to 1,600 Mexicans were killed and as many wounded is simply untrue.

Militarily, the action was small and did not hinder Santa Anna unduly; in other ways its effects were incalculable. The epic defence, perhaps especially the death of the national hero Crockett, caused public opinion in the United States to swing wholly behind the Texians in terms of support, volunteers, matériel and cash. Verses published by the New Orleans *Commercial Bulletin* reflected the outrage of the USA:

> Vengeance on Santa Anna and his minions,
> Vile scum, up boiled from the infernal
>   regions . . .
> The offscouring baseness of hell's
>   blackest legions,
> Too filthy far with crawling worms to
>   dwell
> And far too horrid and too base for hell.

Houston's 'Runaway Scrape'

Realising the need to concentrate whatever forces were available, Houston found 374 men gathered at Gonzales on 11 March, including Neill, Burleson and Sidney Sherman, leader of a company of Kentucky volunteers. Houston had intended to join Fannin in a relief of the Alamo; news of its fall—confirmed when Houston's legendary scout 'Deaf' Smith returned with Mrs Dickinson—decided him to order a retreat before Gen. Sesma, who was even then advancing on Gonzales with 700 men. The Texian withdrawal east—known as the 'Runaway Scrape'—has suffered from selective interpretations arising out of political bias surrounding Houston's later career. Strategically, it was a wise withdrawal, as the 'colonies' across the Colorado River offered vital supplies and reinforcements. As Houston reported, his 374 men were 'without two days provisions, many without arms, others without ammunition . . . remote from succour, it would have been madness to have hazarded a contest . . . I . . . had succeeded in organising the troops, but the first principles of drill had not been taught to them . . . By falling back, Texas can rally. . . .' In other

Interior of the Alamo chapel. (The Alamo Museum)

words, as he had written to Fannin in November: 'Remember our maxim, it is better to do well late than never.'

Nonetheless, the withdrawal was unpopular; one unhappy volunteer remarked, as the dependants were being evacuated from Gonzales with the army, 'we are all looking out for Number One'. Included in the eastward flight was the government, leaving Washington-on-the-Brazos ('a disgusting place . . . about a dozen wretched cabins') for Harrisburg. The newly elected provisional President, David Burnet, was a stern man with no liking for profanity or alcohol. This augured ill for his relations with Houston, who nicknamed him 'Wetumpka' which (he said) was Cherokee for 'hog thief'.

Fannin at La Bahía

At La Bahía (Goliad) lay Fannin with Texas's best force, drilled (albeit unwillingly) and adequately equipped, comprising the Georgia and Lafayette battalions of infantry (both formed of independent companies) and an artillery detachment, the majority being US volunteers. Fannin squandered his resources. He sent Capt. King's company to Refugio to evacuate civilians; but they were overrun as Urrea's division moved north towards La Bahía, and King and seven or eight others who lived to surrender were tied to trees and shot. Fannin then sent Maj. Ward's Georgia battalion to find King; they, too, were attacked and surrendered. Reduced to about 300 dismounted men and 25 cavalry, Fannin destroyed his fortifications, spiked his heavy guns, and marched from La Bahía to join Houston.

Encumbered by baggage, he halted on the open prairie, when a further two miles would have brought him to water (the Coleto River) and the protection of timber. In this exposed position he was caught by a large Mexican force. Fannin formed a hollow square with artillery at the corners, and repulsed a cavalry charge which came almost within bayonet range; Fannin's own cavalry, which had been scouting, had bolted when the Mexicans appeared. An incessant sharpshooting continued until nightfall, with the Texians' Kentucky rifles

wreaking havoc. During the night Fannin's men erected a breastwork of earth and baggage around their position; but on the morning of 20 March the Mexicans received reinforcements, including two cannon. Out of artillery ammunition, Fannin gave his men a choice: attempt to fight their way out or surrender. Some, like the company of Alabama Red Rovers, were for fighting, come what may; but it was decided that the 70 Texian wounded could not be abandoned (only about ten had been killed). Fannin, himself shot in the thigh, surrendered on the promise of fair treatment, and the force returned to La Bahía.

Also confined at La Bahía were the prisoners from the Georgia Bn., and a boat-load of volunteers captured at Copano, these last being ordered to wear a white cloth around their arms, for a reason which became apparent. A Mexican Act of 1835 had decreed death to all foreigners taken under arms in Texas. From a legalistic point of view,

'Travis defends the wall of the Alamo': a typical example of how the Alamo has been portrayed in later art, and how it has come to be regarded in some quarters as the very symbol of liberty. Some later reconstructions exhibit considerable inaccuracy, especially in the costume of the Mexican army. This is one of the better examples of the genre. Painting by Ruth Conerly Zachrisson. (The Alamo Museum)

Urrea and his officers treated the prisoners correctly. They saved several dozen of Fannin's men who had been colonists from Refugio and San Patricio (not foreigners); the Copano prisoners (not taken in arms); and medical personnel, to care for the Mexican wounded. On Santa Anna's orders, the remainder were marched out on the early morning of Palm Sunday, 27 March, being told they were to be paroled to New Orleans. A little way from Goliad their escorts opened fire; only about 30 escaped. Some 342 prisoners (by Texian reckoning) were thus murdered: 'a day of most heartfelt sorrow,' as one Mexican officer wrote, 'the prisoners were all young and of fine florid complexions'. Immobilised by his wound, Fannin was carried from his room and shot with the rest of the invalids.

Houston's little force was now left as the only resistance to the subjugation of Texas. Morale sank as the eastward withdrawal continued through torrential rain, and a rumour started that Houston intended to march to Louisiana and involve the USA. But at Groce's Plantation, across the Brazos, Houston began to turn his rabble into an army. He had formed one regiment under Burleson at Gonzales; now he organised a second under Sidney Sherman, who had sold his business in Kentucky to

Most depictions of the assault on the Alamo are inaccurate; this version is among the best, with a reasonable degree of accuracy in the depiction of the palisade connecting the chapel with the Low Barracks; the Mexicans are shown in 'open' columns. The main error is that the scene appears to be full daylight, whereas the actual assault took place at dawn. Detail of a print after Theodore Gentilz, 1844.

equip his own company for Texas. For two weeks the Texians drilled and re-equipped; more volunteers arrived, bringing the total to about 800 under arms, with two 6 pdr. cannon donated by the citizens of Cincinnati, christened the 'Twin Sisters' and commanded by James Neill. A mounted scouting troop was established under Capt. H. Karnes, including the redoubtable 'Deaf' Smith.

Dissent at Houston's tactics almost led to mutiny, forestalled by a threat of execution for any man who followed the appeal of Mirabeau Buonaparte Lamar, a Georgia publisher and poet, to go off in search of Mexicans; instead, Lamar accepted command of Houston's cavalry. President Burnet demanded Houston fight, and prepared to depose him; Houston ignored it all, waiting for Santa Anna's communications to lengthen. As he said, 'I consulted none . . . If I err, the blame is mine.'

Santa Anna divided his forces: Gaona's division went north from San Antonio, Urrea south from Goliad to Matagorda and Brazoria, while he himself took 750 of Sesma's reinforced command, intending to reunite at Fort Bend. Leaving Sesma to follow, Santa Anna pushed on in an attempt to capture the Texian government at Harrisburg, which fled before him to New Washington and Galveston. But Santa Anna had out-distanced his supports, the error for which Houston had been waiting.

Finding the Texian government had eluded him by moments, Santa Anna turned to attack Houston, telling his generals at Fort Bend to come up without delay. By a 60-mile forced march in two and a half days, Houston came within range just before noon on 18 April. Learning that Santa Anna was at New Washington, Houston determined to strike before Mexican reinforcements could arrive. Calling to his ragged army, 'Victory is certain! Trust in God and fear not! The victims of the Alamo and the names of those who were murdered at Goliad cry out for vengeance!' Houston gave the Texians their war-cry: 'Remember the Alamo! Remember Goliad!' Crossing to the Harrisburg side

Susannah Dickinson and her infant daughter Angelina leave the ruins of the Alamo after the assault, watched by Mexican infantry; the surviving non-combatants were treated with courtesy by the Mexican officers. Holding the horse is Col. Almonte's orderly, an American Negro named Ben, who was deputed to act as Mrs Dickinson's escort from the Alamo, and who later became Houston's servant. He is not to be confused with Travis's slave, Joe, another Alamo survivor who joined Mrs Dickinson on her flight from the Alamo. Painting by H. A. De Young. (The Alamo Museum)

of Buffalo Bayou, Houston withdrew his men to the protection of woods by the San Jacinto River on 20 April, and awaited the Mexicans.

San Jacinto

Santa Anna was reinforced on the morning of 21 April by Gen. Cós, who had hurried up from Fort Bend, bringing the Mexican strength to 1,250 or 1,300 men, with a single fieldpiece (probably a 6- or 9-pdr.) and little cavalry. Included were the Guerrero, Aldama, Matamoros and Toluca Bns., two companies of the Guadalajara, and the preference companies of the 1st Mexico City— none, ironically, were the executioners of La Bahía. Their position was strong, for during the night a barricade of supplies and pack-saddles had been erected on the plain of San Jacinto, before the Texian camp.

As 21 April dragged towards noon, more criticism came from the Texian ranks; Houston asked some if they wanted a fight. When they replied with a shout, he told them to eat their dinners first, then sent 'Deaf' Smith to destroy Vince's Bridge and prevent further reinforcements reaching Santa Anna. He assembled the army: Lamar's cavalry, screened by woods on the right; then Burleson's First Regiment, with Sherman's Second on the left flank, with the 'Twin Sisters', three fifes and a drum in the centre. The Mexicans were taking their siesta, Santa Anna was asleep (possibly aided by opium), and none were expecting an action so late in the day. Ordering his men into line and to trail arms, Houston began his advance at about 4.30 pm on 21 April 1836.

The Texians advanced in silence within 200 yards of the Mexican breastworks; apparently some riflemen had been thrown forward and came into action first, with the 'Twin Sisters' firing in the centre, and the musicians playing 'Will you come to the bower?' a popular ballad. Houston tried to preserve discipline, crying 'Halt, halt . . . God damn you, fire! Aren't you going to fire at all?' Sixty yards from the breastwork, as the Mexicans sleepily ran to their positions and began to fire, 'Deaf' Smith galloped up shouting 'Fight for your lives! Vince's Bridge is down!' As the pace increased, all cohesion was lost, the men firing and loading as they ran, always crying 'Remember the Alamo! Remember Goliad!' It was an unleashing of suppressed rage, of vengeance without mercy, as the following Texian letter shows:

'... have done your heart good to see them fall ... the most delightful time that ever I heard since the world commenced. I had a first rate Rifle ... Betsy would bore a hole in them the Claret would gush out as large as a corn stalk one big fellow ... I shot in the neck it appeared that it had near cut his head off. I shot old Betsy 6 times and a large holster pistol one time ... I no that I killed four that thing I no ... I shot that fellow in the left eye plum ... it seemed to do me more good at that time to have shot or a bayonet run through them than any thing I have ever yet seen ...'

Houston's horse fell dead, and a bullet shattered his leg, but he remounted and took the barricade. The Mexican flanks crumbled as Lamar's cavalry swept from cover on to their left, and Sherman fell on their right. Santa Anna claimed that when he awoke he attempted to rally the Aldama, and to form a column of counter-attack from the Guerrero and the picquets of the Toluca and Guadalajara;

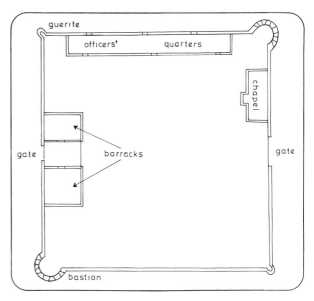

Plan of Presidio La Bahía (Goliad): a typical frontier fort. The corners were defended alternately by *guerites* (sentry-boxes on the ramparts) and bastions, the latter designed to mount a cannon, with five embrasures cut to allow enfilade attacks on any of the four faces of the fort.

The chapel at Presidio La Bahía: Fannin was executed in front of this building. (Kevin R. Young)

The outer walls and corner bastion of Presidio La Bahía. (Kevin R. Young)

but the Mexicans were already fleeing, and the butchery began. Around the barricade the Texians wielded their rifles as clubs; 'Deaf' Smith killed a Mexican with his own sabre, then slew another with a blow so violent that it snapped the blade. Gen. Manuel Castrillon tried to rally some Mexicans by jumping on to an ammunition box, where he stood with folded arms, glaring at the Texians: 'I've been in forty battles and never showed my back. I'm too old to do it now!' Texian Secretary-at-War Col. Rusk tried to save Castrillon, 'a Castillian gentleman', but the Texians were out of control, and shot him to pieces. Santa Anna fled, as did most surviving Mexicans; Texian officers tried to stop the butchery, but as one was told by a volunteer, 'If Jesus Christ were to come down from heaven and order me to quit shooting Santanistas, I wouldn't do it, sir!'

The battle was over in 18 minutes; out of 783 Texians, two were killed and 23 wounded, six mortally. Some 600 Mexicans were slaughtered and about 730 taken prisoner. The latter, herded together by Rusk, threw alarm into Houston who believed them to be Mexican reinforcements; for, as he said, a hundred disciplined troops could have routed the Texians, who had run mad with revenge. The cry '*Me no Alamo!*' and '*Me no Goliad!*', even if true, gave little protection from the hands of the enraged Texians. The Alamo and the Fannin massacre had been avenged in a welter of blood.

Santa Anna was captured in disguise on the following day; but Houston let him live, recognising that he was vital in securing peace—or at least a respite. Over the next few weeks Santa Anna succeeded in avoiding several impromptu lynching-parties called in his honour. To save his life he agreed on an armistice which 'Deaf' Smith and Burleson transmitted to the Mexican army at Fort Bend; upon its receipt they marched out of Texas. The Mexican government repudiated the peace; but, in effect, the 18 minutes slaughter at San Jacinto had won independence for Texas. Santa Anna eventually re-established his despotic rule in Mexico, and sporadic hostilities continued for a decade, until the Republic of Texas was taken into the United States and Mexican claims were ended by the US-Mexican War of 1846.

'It was but a small affair' is how Santa Anna described the storming of the Alamo. In military terms, it was; but its effect, and that of the execution of Fannin's command, was profound, helping to shape the future of US-Mexican relations and, in 'Remember the Alamo', providing history with one of its more memorable slogans. The Mexicans were probably as much the victims of Santa Anna's malevolence as were the Texians; for it was the Mexican soldiery which paid the price of Texian revenge, not the architect of their misfortune. In seeking a last word on the victims of the Alamo, of Goliad—and of San Jacinto—perhaps the most appropriate comes from Rusk's oration at the burial of Fannin's command: 'While liberty has a habitation and a name, their chivalrous deeds will be handed down upon the bright pages of history.'

The Mexican Army

Years of political upheaval had left the Mexican army in disorder. It consisted of two categories: the regular army (*Ejercito permanente*); and the territorial militia (*Milicia activa*) who, having been on active duty for some years, were practically regulars. In the autumn of 1835 the Mexican army listed theoretical battalions and regiments where, in reality, only companies existed. A re-organisation was in progress, and before the end of 1835 a new army was formed, partially trained and equipped.

Soldiers were either volunteers on eight-year enlistment, or conscripts serving ten years. The average soldier was usually between 5 ft. and 5 ft. 6 ins. in height; at 5 ft. 10 ins., Santa Anna was one of the tallest men in the army. Discipline, by European standards, was lax; for example, only in 1847 was the saluting of superiors made compulsory. The army was styled upon Spanish lines; but the rapidity with which the force for Texas was raised resulted in some cases in deplorable standards, with some units under strength and untrained. (Lt.Col. José de la Peña described the Yucatán Battalion, who were late reinforcements, as composed of Mayan Indians, 'aborigines . . . did not know the language and could hardly handle a musket'.) The set regulations for manoeuvre (with all commands transmitted by bugle-call) can only have been effective with trained troops; and the lack of experience of much of the Mexican army led to the failure in picqueting which resulted in the débâcle of San Jacinto.

The ten regular battalions of infantry were formed by December 1835 by the re-organisation of the previously numbered battalions, as follows, the names being those of heroes of the War of Independence: the Hidalgo Bn. was formed from the old 1st and 2nd Bns.; Allende from the 3rd; Morelos from the 4th; Guerrero from the 5th; Aldama from the 6th; Jiménez from the 7th and 12th; Landero from the 8th and 9th; Matamoros from the 10th; Abasolo from the 11th; and Galeana from the 13th. Each battalion comprised six companies of fusiliers and one each of grenadiers and chasseurs or light infantry; in European fashion, these élite or 'preference' companies could be detached and formed into *ad hoc* grenadier or chasseur battalions, as (for example) in the storming of the Alamo. In addition to the regular and militia battalions there were eight 'standing companies' (Acapulco, San Blas, Tampico, 1st and 2nd Bacalar, Carmen Island, 1st and 2nd Tabasco); and a decree of May 1824 was revived in 1835 to designate some regular and militia units to be light infantry, each of eight companies including one of sharpshooters. Actual strengths in the Texas campaign appear to have borne little resemblance to the official establishments. At San Luis Potosi in December 1835, the strongest battalion (San Luis) numbered 452 effectives, and the weakest (Tres Villas) only 189; the average strength of the nine battalions listed in these returns (including only one regular, the Jiménez) was 344. Company strengths averaged between 58 (San Luis) and 34 men.

The cavalry similarly consisted of regulars and militia. By December 1835 six regular regiments (named after battlefields of the revolution against Spain) had been formed from the previous units: the Dolores Regt. from the old 3rd and 6th Regts.;

Joseph March Chadwick, Fannin's adjutant at La Bahía, and one of the Texian army's drill instructors. A West Point 'drop-out', he had previously served as aide to the Governor of Illinois during the Black Hawk War. (Kevin R. Young)

Iguala from the 4th and 10th; Palamar from the 2nd, 7th and the Active Regt. of Mexico; Cuautla from the 11th and 12th; Veracruz from the 5th and 9th; and Tampico from the 1st and 8th. There were also independent regular units in the Yucatán Sqn. and Tabasco Company. Each regiment comprised four squadrons of two companies each, with a squad of pioneers attached to regimental headquarters. Some regulars were converted to light cavalry in 1835. Drill and manoeuvre were copied from Spanish models, but in practice were applied only sporadically.

The *Zapadores* (engineer corps) was regarded as the army's élite, although in December 1835 only 185 in number; with the detached grenadiers, they formed the reserve for the assault on the Alamo.

The campaign of San Jacinto, showing troop movements of Houston's Texian army (dotted line) and the Mexican forces (broken line). The crossed swords symbol near Lynchburg denotes the field of San Jacinto.

The artillery also seems to have been of a higher standard than the average Mexican unit; it was deployed piecemeal through the army rather than concentrated as a central battery. Transport and supply, on the other hand, were chaotic. Santa Anna financed the war by loans on outrageous terms (at interest of 48 per cent per annum), and all administration was riddled with corruption. For example, Gen. Gaona personally cornered the supplies along the army's route and sold them to the army at double the price; the master-purveyor, Santa Anna's brother-in-law Col. Ricardo Dromundo, never even accounted for the money he received, and even sold bedding at extortionate prices to the Mexican wounded. Not until August 1836 was a Military Health Corps established; even Texian prisoners had to be recruited as medical orderlies, and Santa Anna's personal surgeon was only a village practitioner. Transport was organised

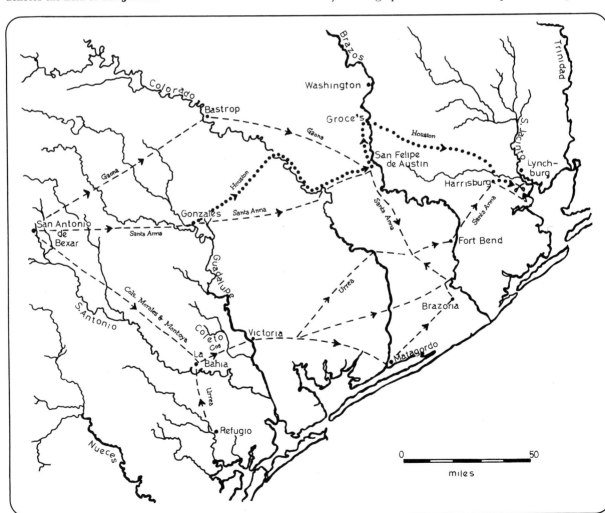

1, 2 & 3:
Texian volunteers, 1835

A

1: Lt. Col. William B. Travis
2: Col. David Crockett
3: Col. James Bowie

B

1: Private, Alabama Red Rovers
2: Private, New Orleans Greys
3: Volunteer, ex-US Army

1   3   2

C

1: Sam Houston
2: Texian cavalry scout
3: Volunteer with 'San Jacinto Battle Flag'
4: Texian volunteer officer

D

1: Gen. Santa Anna, campaign dress
2: Mexican Gen. of Bde., full dress
3: Mexican staff officer, Commandancies
   of Fortified Places, full dress
4: Captain, Mexican Reserve Cavalry

E

1: Sergeant, Mexican Regular Cavalry
2: Trooper, Mexican Light Cavalry
3: Sapper, Mexican Regular Cavalry

F

1: Cpl., Mexican Tres Villas Inf. Bn.
2: 1st Sgt., Mexican Matamoros Inf. Bn.
3: Grenadier, Mexican Infantry
4: Fusilier, Mexican Infantry

G

1: Officer, Mexican Infantry
2: Private, Mexican Light Infantry
3: Lancer, Mexican Presidial companies
4: Mexican artilleryman

at unit level, the line of march being hopelessly encumbered by sutlers and *soldaderas* (female camp-followers), disruptive to military order but necessary to supplement the meagre commissariat arrangements.

Though ill-fed, ill-equipped, ill-trained and neglected, the Mexican soldier was not always ill-led. A hard core of senior officers were assiduous, experienced professionals like Lt.Col. de la Peña of the *Zapadores*; or Europeans like Gen. Vincente Filisola, an Italian who had served in the Spanish army, and Adrian Woll, an ex-Napoleonic French officer. But though many officers were veterans, others were useless political appointees; the Secretary of State complained in April 1834 of the 'prodigality of ranks and decorations conferred on a multitude that does not know how to lead . . . as a result of this disorder, well trained and punctilious

---

Mexican Order of Battle

There were changes in the Mexican order of battle, and in unit strengths, throughout the campaign, as units were re-assigned for specific tasks and suffered the varying fortunes of war. Sources inevitably conflict; we know, however, that in mid-December 1835 the Army of Operations for Texas was arranged as follows:

1st Division (or 'Vanguard Bde.')
Gen. Joaquim Ramirez y Sesma
Permanent Bns. Matamoros (272 men), Jiménez (274); Active Bn. San Luis Potosi (452); Permanent Regt. Dolores Cavalry (290); 62 artillerymen with two 8-pdrs., two 6-pdrs., two 4-pdrs., one 7-pdr. howitzer (*or a total of eight guns?*)

2nd Division
Gen. Santa Anna
1st Bde.: Gen. Antonio Gaona
Permanent Bn. Aldama (393); Active Bns. Toluca (324), Queretaro (375), San Luis Potosi (detachment, 31), Guanajuato (391); 63 artillerymen with two 12-pdrs., two 6-pdrs., two 4-pdrs.
2nd Bde.: Gen. Eugenio Tolsa
Permanent Bn. Guerrero (403); Active Bns. Mexico City (363), Guadalajara (428); 60 artillerymen with two 8-pdrs., two 4-pdrs., two 7-pdr. howitzers

Cavalry
Gen. Juan José de Andrade
Permanent Regts. Tampico (250), Cuautla (180); Active Regts. Guanajuato (180), San Luis Potosi (40), Bajio (30); one 4-pdr. gun (?)

Zapadores
Lt.Col. Augustin Amat, with 185 men

In early January 1836, Urrea's force comprised the Cuautla Regt. and the newly joined Active Bn. Yucatán, and detachments of the San Luis Potosi and Bajio Cavalry. Santa Anna's force was re-organised thus at the Rio Grande:

1st Bde.: Gen. Gaona
Bns. Aldama, Toluca, Queretaro and Guanajuato; *Zapadores*; some presidial troops; six guns
2nd Bde.: Gen. Tolsa
Bns. Morelos, Guerrero, Mexico City, Guadalajara and Tres Villas; six guns
Cavalry Bde.: Gen. Andrade
Regts. Tampico and Guanajuato

The force besieging the Alamo comprised the Matamoros, San Luis Potosi, Aldama, Toluca and Jiménez Bns.; *Zapadores*, some cavalry and artillery, under Sesma. Gaona and the rest of the 1st Bde. arrived after the battle, followed by Gens. Tolsa and Andrade. On 11 March, Sesma took the Aldama, Matamoros and Toluca Bns., with Dolores and Tampico Cavalry, on the advance on San Felipe; Col. Morales led the Jiménez and San Luis Potosi Bns. to reinforce Urrea. Tolsa led part of the Guerrero and the Mexico City Bn. to reinforce Sesma; Col. Montoya was sent with the remainder of the Guerrero and the Tres Villas Bn. to reinforce Urrea. Morales joined up with Urrea before the battle of the Coleto, and Montoya on the day before the Goliad massacre.

On the 'Runaway Scrape': Houston dictates orders to his aide, George W. Hockley. Engraving from *Sam Houston and his Republic* (**1846**).

officers have retired from the service . . .' For example, between December 1835 and May 1836 the Tres Villas Bn. suffered four changes of command until it devolved upon a German engineer, Col. J. J. Holsinger; like his predecessors he later abandoned his command, and the battalion was taken over by a captain. Its colonel, Alcérrica, was charged with deserting his post, and feigned dementia to escape punishment!

Nevertheless, the overall standard of the army was such that it impressed some contemporary observers, such as Capt. Reuben M. Potter, who noted that it contained many European and American soldiers of experience.

In addition there were the local forces, 'presidial' companies which garrisoned the frontier *presidios*; cavalry augmented by local inhabitants. Most of these stayed loyal; the San Antonio presidial company, for example, appears to have served with

Cós, while others from the area formed Seguin's company of the Texian forces. The split is demonstrated by the Esparza family of San Antonio; Gregorio Esparza died defending the Alamo, while his brother, in the San Antonio presidial company, joined Santa Anna.

Mexican Uniforms

As with organisation, drill and equipment, Mexican uniforms followed Spanish lines, confirmed by the dress regulations of 1821, 1823 and 1827; but years of chaos and neglect led to troops being ill-supplied and wearing styles which were officially obsolete. It is thus difficult to be precise about exactly what uniform was worn by the Mexican army in the Texas war; the rapidity with which the army was assembled would have resulted in regiments receiving whatever was available, so that different styles may even have been used within the same unit.

In January 1832 an attempt was made to standardise the uniform of the army, which 'becomes more difficult every day because of the confusion in which it finds itself'. Infantry were to receive every 30 months a blue coatee with scarlet collar, cuffs and lapels, white piping, coarse lining and yellow buttons; two sailcloth jackets and trousers, two linen shirts, two velveteen stocks, two pairs of shoes and a forage-cap. Every 60 months they were to be issued an overcoat, a leather shako with brass plate and chinscales, cotton cords and pompon, and a hide or canvas knapsack with leather straps. Also issued was a cartridge box with tin interior and leather belt, a canteen with strap, and a burlap blanket with leather straps; in 1835 an extra shirt, shoulder belt, tool-kit, towel, bayonet and scabbard and one pair each of full dress, cloth and canvas trousers are noted.

In June 1833 the uniform was amended to a single-breasted dark blue coatee with red collar, cuffs, flaps and piping but no lapels, with the unit number embroidered upon the collar; and dark blue or white canvas trousers. The 1832 (lapelled) and 1833 (single-breasted) coatees appear to have been worn indiscriminately, though the intermixture of styles created conflicting evidence. Turnbacks were red for both, the piping white for 1832 and red for 1833, and shoulder straps dark blue with red piping, though crimson epaulettes without fringes seem to have been used with the 1833 pattern at least. 'Preference' companies (grenadiers and chasseurs) wore a vertical flash or *sardineta* on the cuff from 1833, though some units used this ornament when not entitled, so that in 1836 an order was issued restricting its use to a single flash for regimental preference companies, and a double flash for the élite companies formed within units consisting entirely of grenadiers or chasseurs. After the 1835 re-organisation, initial letters may have been borne on the collar in place of the earlier number: e.g. 'BM' for *Battalón Matamoros*, etc. Similar initials seem to have been borne on some accoutrements, such as belt plates, e.g. 'BGO' for *Battalón Guerrero*.

The black leather shako was slightly bell-topped, with red or yellow lace ornamenting the upper edge, and bore the universal national tricolour cockade of red, white and green, with a pompon of red; green (for light infantry); or the national green/white/red design established in November 1821. It had brass chinscales and plate, either an oval bearing the national coat of arms and unit designation, a grenade for grenadiers, or a more elaborate coat of arms. Cotton cords and raquettes were specified in 1832, omitted in 1833 but listed again in 1835: yellow for fusiliers, red for grenadiers and green for chasseurs, so presumably their use was not universal. Contrary to some modern depictions, the shako did *not* have a tricoloured 'target' on the top surface, this being a misinterpretation of Linate's prints of 1820.

Field officers wore bicorn hats, with tricoloured feathers a distinction of senior officers; regimental officers had to wear the shako or helmet when serving with their unit, but were permitted a plain bicorn without lace or plume on other occasions.

Greatcoats were supposedly issued to regular units, and are shown by some contemporary sources as dark blue, single-breasted garments with six brass buttons, and a red collar, cuffs and piping. The fatigue jacket was a single-breasted, white, sleeved waistcoat, often shown with red collar and cuffs. Trousers of dark blue, or blue-grey with red piping, or white, would have been worn in Texas depending upon availability.

Uniforms of the Active Militia were in an even more parlous state than those of the regulars, though officially they were identical. In 1828 the

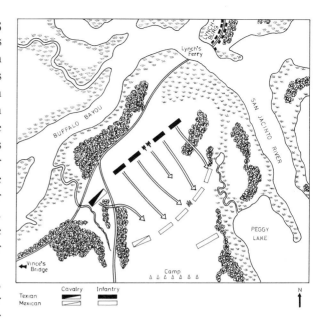

Battle of San Jacinto, 21 April 1836.

regulations of the Coahuila-Texas Militia even stated that 'no militiaman shall be compelled to wear uniforms even in actual service, but . . . he must not be without a cockade, equipment, and the necessary arms'. The 1834 regulations made the possession of a uniform 'discretional as long as the militia can afford them. . . . Its acquisition will be considered a laudable and patriotic deed.'

Rank markings were specified by regulations of January 1830, epaulettes being gold lace for infantry and silver for cavalry in the regular army, and silver for infantry and gold for cavalry in the Active Militia. All officers wore bright red silk waist sashes. The regulations specified:

Colonel: Two epaulettes with bullion fringes, embroidered strap bearing star of contrasting colour (i.e. gold on silver, silver on gold).

Lieutenant-Colonel: As colonel, without the star.

First Adjutant (Major): As lieutenant-colonel, but smooth lace strap; all the above had tricolour hat-feathers and transverse epaulette-loops of five-strand lace.

Captain: Two epaulettes with plain strap, fringe instead of bullion, and transverse strap of the same material as the coatee.

Lieutenant and Second Adjutant: As captain, but epaulette on right shoulder only.

Sub-lieutenant, Sub-adjutant and Ensign: As captain, but epaulette on left shoulder only.

1st Sergeant and Cornet-major: Two silk epaulettes,

crimson for infantry and green for cavalry in the regulars; crimson strap with green fringe for militia infantry, green strap with crimson fringe for militia cavalry.

2nd Sergeant: As 1st sergeant, but epaulette on right shoulder only. (All NCO epaulettes had transverse straps of the epaulette colour.)

Corporal: Retained the 1823 diagonal rank-bar of white or yellow lace on the forearm, and carried a wooden switch with which to belabour privates.

Infantry equipment consisted of white leather cross belts, supporting a black leather cartridge box and bayonet, with the blue-grey blanket rolled atop the knapsack. Weaponry was often in poor

'Come and Take It': a flag of Texian defiance, flown over the Gonzales cannon when the colonists resisted a Mexican attempt to repossess the gun on 1 October 1835. The flag was made by two Gonzales women, Sarah Seely and Evaline DeWitt, from Evaline's wedding dress, with a cannon barrel, star and motto painted in black. (*Bottom*) Texian flag which reputedly flew over the Alamo: the tricolour of Mexico (green/white/red) with the black numerals '1824' replacing the Mexican arms on the white centre, symbolising adherence to the Constitution of that date. A similar design bore two stars instead of the numbers, representing the Mexican states of Texas and Coahuila. Alternatively, one Alamo flag may have been based upon the US Stars and Stripes, with a single white star and the word TEXAS in the blue canton.

condition, the only arms factory in Mexico having ceased production. The majority of weapons were imported from Britain, mainly 'Brown Bess' muskets, probably Tower-manufactured India Patterns (some of which seem to have been condemned as unserviceable in England) along with quantities of carbines and Baker rifles, the latter probably complete with their brass-hilted sword bayonets. Rifles were probably issued to selected troops—light infantry and chasseurs—but it is difficult to be precise as the term *escopeta* appears to have been used indiscriminately for rifles, smoothbored or rifled carbines, or even muskets.

The 1832 regulations specified that cavalrymen should receive every 30 months a coatee with coarse lining, a pair of cloth overalls with leather lining, a pair of cloth trousers for dismounted duty, a sailcloth fatigue jacket and trousers, two linen shirts, two velveteen stocks, a pair of shoes and a forage cap. Every 60 months they were to be issued a cloth cape; and a leather helmet with brass shield, comb and chinscales (white metal is often shown), a goat hair crest (or bearskin, or a horsehair mane as shown in Plate F2), and tricoloured woollen plume or pompon. The short red coatee worn by regular cavalry had green collar, cuffs, turnbacks and piping, and white buttons; the campaign overalls were of 'foxed' grey cloth, and the trousers for dismounted duty of blue cloth, both with a red stripe. The cloak was yellow with a green collar. The territorial (militia) cavalry wore similar uniforms but in reversed colours: green coatee with red collar, cuffs, piping and turnbacks, white buttons, and red shabraques. Accounts which mention the Mexican cavalry wearing cuirasses 'polished armor glistening in the rays of the sun' as seen by John Sutherland, seem to be in error, the impression probably being caused by the sun striking helmet plates and badges.

The Texian Army

The concept of the Texian army as a group of frontiersmen is in part erroneous. Some of the settlers, and many of those who journeyed to Texas to participate in the war, came from a background in which local militia training was familiar, and a considerable number had some military experience.

To a degree, organisation depended upon the number of men which each company commander could enlist, though some units were later amalgamated or augmented to equalise company strengths. It was intended to form the army upon conventional lines, Houston attempting to introduce complete regulations: 'You will proceed to enlist men for the Regular Army of Texas; you will enlist men for two years or for during the war. The pay, rations, clothing &c. will be the same that was allowed during the last war with the U. States,' i.e. 'the same that was established by the U. States during the war with England'. As decreed in November 1835 the regular army consisted of a regiment of artillery and one of infantry, each of two battalions, each battalion comprising five companies of 56 men each. In the infantry each battalion was to have a colonel, a lieutenant-colonel and a major, and each company a captain, a second-lieutenant, four sergeants and four corporals; the artillery likewise, save for two lieutenant-colonels and two majors per battalion, and a third-lieutenant in each company. The whole force was to number 1,120, the artillery also being trained as infantry, and the infantry 'exercised in the rifle as well as infantry service'. Volunteer units from the USA were to be accepted with similar organisation, each company of two platoons of 28 rank-and-file, two sergeants and two corporals, with two musicians per company.

In practice, organisation was much looser, as typified by W. P. Zuber's account of joining Capt. Bennett's company in March 1836. This 'infantry' company originally consisted of about 12 men, of whom eight were mounted; 'though unmilitary', as Zuber noted, it was a common feature. He describes the army as consisting of three companies of volunteer cavalry; three companies of regular infantry, all on foot; and 20-odd companies of volunteer infantry, of whom between half and three-quarters of each company were mounted. Though the infantry fought on foot, when marching the mounted men rode together, and the 'footmen' walked by company. This disorganisation seems typical of the Texian forces throughout the war; but, despite a lack of discipline which resulted in a continual drift to and from the army upon the whim of the individual, when action was near—as

Flag of the New Orleans Greys, captured at the Alamo, reputedly as it flew over the barracks, by Lt. José Maria Torres, who was killed in the act of seizing it. Blue silk with black lettering and gold fringe.

Ehrenberg of the New Orleans Greys wrote at the siege of San Antonio—'I never heard a single order . . . our own consciousness of being able to do something against despotism . . . kept order and discipline in our ranks.'

Attempts were made to instill sufficient drill to enable rudimentary manoeuvres to be performed by those members of the Texian army who had served in some military capacity. Numbers had experience of active service, even in the Napoleonic Wars (e.g. the supposed Alamo survivor, Louis Rose, who had served in Napoleon's army; and one of Fannin's men appears to have served as an English naval gunner at Trafalgar). In addition, the Texian army attracted serving US Army personnel who deserted to go to Texas; Noah Smithwick noted a number present at San Jacinto, and later a US officer sent to reclaim deserters found some 200 still wearing US uniform, most of whom refused to return. The Texian forces were supplied with copies of Scott's *Infantry Tactics*; and among those who instituted regular drill were two members of the Georgia Bn., Joseph M. Chadwick (a West Point drop-out, and aide to the Governor of Illinois in the Black Hawk War) and John S. Brooks (previously a US Marine from the USS *Constitution*). Brooks wrote in January 1836: 'It is nothing but drill every day until I have become completely sick of it.' He was echoed by a Kentucky Mustang who said that drills 'were my detestation and from which

The 'San Jacinto Flag', carried by Sidney Sherman's Kentuckians at the battle of San Jacinto, and the only Texian flag at the action. White ground (now faded to yellow) bearing a painting of the Goddess of Liberty (in natural colours, with black hair), wearing a white Grecian dress with dark red cloak around her legs, with a greyish (blue?) ribbon bearing the black inscription LIBERTY OR DEATH suspended from her sword; all upon a background of dark grey clouds. See Plate D3.

I invariably absented myself,' preferring deer-hunting and fandangoes instead! Nevertheless, the efforts of the drillmasters seem to have given the Texian army the ability to perform a limited degree of orderly manoeuvre.

Fannin's command included the Tampico Artillery, a Mexican company which joined the anti-Santanista forces during an abortive attack on Tampico; not wanting to fight their brethren, the company was discharged at its own request when Santa Anna arrived at San Antonio, and joined Urrea south of Refugio.

Texian Uniforms

Though Houston received a book of US Army uniform details from Capt. Bonnell, commander of Fort Jesup on the US/Texas border (whom Houston unsuccessfully tried to recruit as his aide), there was, with the exception of such volunteer units as the New Orleans Greys and the Alabama Red Rovers, little 'uniformity' about the clothing of the Texian forces. Their initial appearance is perhaps best described by Noah Smithwick:

'Words are inadequate to convey an impression of the appearance of the first Texas army as it formed in marching order. Nothing short of ocular demonstration could do it justice. It certainly bore little resemblance to the army of my childhood dreams. Buckskin breeches were the nearest approach to uniform, and there was a wide diversity even there, some being new and soft and yellow, while others, from long familiarity with rain and grease and dirt, had become hard and black, and shiny. Some, from having passed through the process of wetting and drying on the wearer while he sat on the ground or a chunk before the campfire, with his knees elevated at an angle of eighty-five degrees, had assumed an advanced position at the knee, followed by a corresponding shortening of the lower front length, exposing shins as guiltless of socks as a Kansas Senator's. Boots being an unknown quantity, some wore shoes and some moccasins. Here a broad-brimmed sombrero overshadowed the military cap at its side; there a tall "beegum" rode familiarly beside a coonskin cap, with the tail hanging down behind, as all well regulated tails should do . . . here a bulky roll of bed quilts jostled a pair of "store" blankets; there the shaggy brown buffalo robe contrasted with a gaily coloured checkered counterpane on which the manufacturer had lavished all the skill of dye and weave known to art . . . in lieu of a canteen, each man carried a Spanish gourd . . . Here a big American horse loomed up over the nimble Spanish pony, there a half-broke mustang pranced beside a sober, methodical mule. A fantastic military array to a casual observer, but the one great purpose animating every heart clothed us in a uniform more perfect in our eyes than was ever donned by regulars on dress parade.'

Later in the war certain items of clothing could be drawn from public stores, though not complete uniforms. Among items sent to Texas from New Orleans in January 1836, 'to supply recruits', were 2,012 pairs of brogans, 400 pairs of boots, 366 jackets and pantaloons, 570 pairs of socks, 846 shirts (includng 24 checked, 18 red flannel and 24 white cotton), 18 satinet waistcoats, 24 'Suits Satinett', 3 'Flushing Pea Coats', 12 Kersey pantaloons and 48 pairs of woollen half-hose.

Initially, each man would have provided his own weapons, from hunting rifles to shotguns (the idea that all were excellent shots and all carried 'Kentucky long rifles' is erroneous). W. P. Zuber noted that only unarmed volunteers could draw a weapon from stores, those with their own guns being ineligible for a replacement. This cost Zuber the chance of participating at San Jacinto: much to his disgust, he was left on guard at camp as his own rifle was worthless, misfiring four or five times for every shot it made, yet prone to spontaneous discharges which endangered anyone near him! Virtually all firearms would have been flintlock, due to the lack of availability and unreliability of percussion weapons.

By mid-December 1835 the Texian forces had accumulated a considerable quantity of captured Mexican matériel, little of it of much use. In the Alamo, for example, were listed seven 4-pdr. cannon, two 6-pdrs., two 3-pdrs., a 9-in. 'culverine' and a 5-in. howitzer. In San Antonio were two more 4-pdrs., four 'large cannon' and two swivel-guns, together with ammunition. Of less value was equipment for a band, '30 useless muskets', seven empty boxes, '1 box cartridges, damp', and 66 hats 'of the company of [presidial] lancers'!

Large quantities of munitions were purchased by the Texian government from the USA: e.g., a consignment of January 1836 included among large quantities of supplies, tools, powder and ammunition, 440 US muskets, 100 carbines, 432 canteens, 200 cartridge boxes and belts, 200 pistols and 150 sabres; six bugles, 20 fifes, nine drums (four bearing eagles, two brass); two telescopes; a 'Standard staff' (three dollars), a Standard (50 cents!) and tassels ($2.50); and 18 drill books. As a result, some units were well equipped with US muskets and accoutrements, for example Capt. Turner's company at San Jacinto. Most of the artillery was captured from Mexico, including some strange pieces such as naval guns mounted upon garrison as well as field carriages. At La Bahía Brooks designed a multi-barrelled volley-gun from old Brown Bess barrels, to defend the gate!

Included in the Texian army were some men of striking appearance, such as Martin Palmer, 'the ring-tailed panther', who wore his hair Indian style under a panther-skin hat; and Robert McAlpin Williamson, a lawyer who recruited a ranger company and served at San Jacinto as a cavalry trooper. An illness had caused his right leg to stiffen into an L-shape, drawn up at the knee, so he attached a peg-leg to his right knee and was known thereafter as 'Three-Legged Willie'.

The Plates

A1, 2 and 3: Texian volunteers, 1835
The three figures in this plate wear their civilian clothes, common to the majority of the Texian forces. One is dressed as a frontiersman, with a 'hunting frock' or 'hunting shirt', a common garment of fabric or buckskin, usually with a yoke across the shoulders and fringed edges, with buckskin Indian leggings and moccasins. Another has 'store clothes': a frock coat and the common 'round hat'. The third wears working clothes, with a haversack acting as a 'hold-all'.

Weaponry varied from Kentucky rifles to

Texian artillery, 1835. Facsimile of the illustration drawn by Noah Smithwick's daughter, from his description, of the 'Come and Take It' cannon mounted upon a home-made carriage with slices of tree-trunk for wheels. Naïvely drawn though it is, and although the cannon would seem to be rather too large in comparison with the ox-team, it is a valuable record of the improvisation necessary among the Texian forces. The driver appears to have a short-barrelled firearm slung on his back.

shotgun fowling pieces and even old blunderbuss-type firearms useful only at close range. Personal equipment was a matter of choice or availability, though the ideal was probably that described by one of the Kentucky Mustangs: a 'good Kentucky rifle', shot pouch, powder horn, tomahawk, butcher knife and knapsack, later augmented by a Mexican blunderbuss. Those experienced with the Kentucky rifle could achieve fine marksmanship: 'It was no unusual thing for many of them to put three balls out of five, at a distance of one hundred yards, into a paper not larger than a silver dollar.' These long-barrelled weapons, characterised by the elegant proportions of a stock often incorporating a decorative brass-lidded patch box, were in fact developed from German *jäger* rifles made by early immigrants to Pennsylvania—but the 'Kentucky' nickname has stuck. They had up to four times the effective range of a common musket, and were remarkably accurate even at 300 yards.

The name 'Mustangs', applied to Capt. Burr H. Duval's volunteer company from Bardstown, Kentucky, had an unusual origin. Their 2nd lieutenant was 'most peaceful and genial' until under the influence of alcohol, when his habit was to kick the door from every Mexican house within range. From his kicking came the name 'Mustang', which was adopted by his entire company! The Mustangs formed part of the Lafayette Battalion.

Shown in this plate is the Gonzales cannon known as 'Come and Take It' (from the legend on the flag which flew over the gun when the Mexicans tried to repossess it). It consisted of an old 22 in.

Alamo cannons, excavated from the site of the defences, and deliberately damaged before being buried, almost certainly by the Mexican army in 1836. The cannon in the background is probably the Alamo's famous 18-pdr.: note how the cascabel has been smashed off. (Kevin R. Young)

iron barrel which fired grapeshot, mounted upon a home-made wooden carriage with four-inch-thick slices of tree-trunk as wheels; though it presumably answered its original function of frightening Indians, militarily its only use was as a symbol of defiance and a rallying-point. Drawn by a yoke of oxen, it was soon abandoned by the Texians.

B1: Lt.Col. William Barret Travis
This plate illustrates the three leading figures in the defence of the Alamo, as they might have appeared just before the commencement of the siege.

William B. Travis (1809–36), the South Carolinian lawyer who had been a member of the 'war party' agitating for independence as early as 1832, was a somewhat flamboyant character, who in civilian life had favoured a white hat and red trousers. He appears to have entertained a conviction that he was destined for immortality: he completed his autobiography at the age of 23! Despite a tendency to dramatise (witnessed by his proclamations from the Alamo) he was unswervingly loyal to his principles; and, when sent to command the regulars in the Alamo with the rank of lieutenant-colonel in the Texian cavalry, he found his opportunity to make the mark upon history which he believed was his destiny.

Travis is shown wearing a typical 'round hat' of the period, and a civilian tail-coat; he had ordered a uniform for himself, but apparently was killed before he could receive it. The Mexican Sgt. Nuñez, who appropriated his coat after the battle, said that it was of home-made Texas jeans.

B2: Col. David Crockett
The most famous of frontiersmen, 'Davy' Crockett (1786–1836), an uneducated Tennessean, established so great a reputation as a hunter, fighter, raconteur and general 'character' that he was half a legend even before his death. He served three terms in the House of Representatives (two as Democrat, one as Whig), and only went to Texas when defeated in 1835. His colonelcy was a courtesy title emanating from the US Militia; in Texas he said he wished only to be a 'high private', and 'to aid you all I can in your noble cause . . . all the honor I desire is that of defending . . . in common with my fellow citizens, the liberties of our common country'. A letter to his children told his attitude to the

Carronade excavated from the site of the Alamo. From the deliberate damage (the left hand trunnion has been smashed off), it would appear that this formed part of the Alamo's artillery reported as 'rendered useless' and buried by Gen. Andrade in 1836. A British gun designed originally for naval warfare, the carronade was a close-quarter piece of quite horrifying power when firing grapeshot. (Kevin R. Young)

desperate situation: 'Do not be uneasy about me. I am among friends.'

Crockett is shown wearing a hunting frock over more conventional shirt and legwear, with the coonskin cap which has become part of the Crockett legend, and which Mrs Dickinson noted lying beside his body just after the battle. His rifle in Texas was his old hunting weapon known as 'Betsey', not the ornate 'Pretty Betsey' presented to him by the Whigs.

One of the enduring mysteries of the Alamo is the story from Mexican sources that Crockett was one of six Texians who attempted to surrender but who were executed on Santa Anna's orders. As they had hidden themselves under some mattresses in one of the barrack rooms, and as Crockett appears to have died where Mrs Dickinson found him, between the church and the Long Barracks, it would appear that he died fighting—as is suggested by everything we know of his character.

B3: Col. James Bowie

Jim Bowie (1796–1836) was famous principally as a duellist and entrepreneur, though commissioned a colonel in the Texian army in December 1835 and appointed to command the volunteers in the Alamo. A living legend who literally carved his reputation with his famous knife (which may, in fact, have been invented by a brother), he had

reputedly made fortunes from land deals and even from slave trading with the pirate Lafitte. He was a courteous, even polished man, and his quiet bearing made him appear even more potentially lethal than his string of famous fights suggested. Though a Mexican citizen from 1830, and married to the daughter of the vice-Governor, he was a leading figure in the early independence movement, and had been involved in several skirmishes in 1835. Devastated by the death of his wife and children from cholera in 1833, Bowie began to drink heavily, and was ailing by the end of 1835. The illness which incapacitated him at the Alamo is uncertain—perhaps tuberculosis, typhoid or pneumonia; but there seems little truth in the story that he was injured by a fall from the ramparts or crushed by a cannon.

C1: Private, Alabama Red Rovers

The Red Rovers were a volunteer company about 61 strong, formed by Dr John Shackelford around Courtland, Alabama. The women of the community made their uniforms: 'linsey woolsey' hunting shirts, fringed on the sleeves and shoulders and dyed bright red (one source also mentions 'brown and green checks'), from which the unit took its name. Their 'full dress' consisted of a cap and jacket of red velvet, white trousers and a blue sash. Equipment of knapsack, haversack, canteen,

Cannon mounted upon a reproduction carriage, Presidio La Bahía. The 'naval' style of carriage is likely to have been used for static ordnance. (Kevin R. Young)

cartridge box and blanket, and US muskets, were furnished by the Alabama State Arsenal. Leaving in December 1835, the Rovers joined Fannin at La Bahía and went into the Lafayette Battalion. Almost all died when the prisoners at La Bahía were shot, though Dr Shackelford was spared to treat Mexican casualties. Included among the murdered was his own son, and, as Dr J. H. Barnard noted, the experience seemed to add ten years to the poor doctor's appearance.

C2: Private, New Orleans Greys

Two companies of New Orleans Greys were enrolled, under Capts. Thomas H. Breece and Robert C. Morris (later William G. Cooke, who served as Houston's aide at San Jacinto); composed of 'mostly athletic mechanics', it was one of the best-equipped volunteer corps from the USA. According to a German recruit, Herman Ehrenberg (late of the University of Jena), Breece's company at least wore 'grey, made-for-service-in-the-prairie-fitting uniforms, which we found ready-made in the numerous magazines' of New Orleans, before their departure for Texas. Illustrated is a Model 1825 forage cap with US equipment and knapsack, worn with the usual impedimenta of knives and civilian belts; doubtless the caps and trousers were replaced in some cases with the prevalent civilian styles. Armed with US muskets or rifles, the unit appeared so impressive that the local Cherokee chief mistook

them for US regulars when they entered Nacogdoches.

The Greys played a leading rôle in the capture of San Antonio, before dividing: one part remained in the Alamo and the other embarked on the abortive Matamoros expedition, returning to join Fannin in La Bahía. In the vanguard with the Alabama Red Rovers at the Coleto fight, the Greys wanted to fight their way out, but Fannin's council prevailed. Ehrenberg was one of the few survivors of the Goliad massacre; about 33 appear to have died in the Alamo. The Greys' flag was traditionally that flying above the Alamo during the final assault. Note 'extra' blunderbuss—a popular close-quarter weapon among Texians and Presidial troops.

C3: Volunteer in US Army uniform

This figure wears items of US uniform, taken with him when deserting from the US Army to join the Texians. Considerable numbers of US deserters swelled the Texian ranks, attracted by the prospect of bounty or action, or from a desire to assist their countrymen in a campaign which was doubtless more attractive than the guerrilla war against the Seminoles. The man illustrated wears a dress coatee of the US artillery, minus epaulettes, though troops on the frontier would have made greater use of the sky-blue kersey undress jacket and trousers of a style not unlike that of the New Orleans Greys. He wears the 1833 leather forage cap (as may conceivably have been worn by the Greys), constructed so as to fold flat; but apart from his musket, the remainder of his 'equipment' is privately acquired.

A fairly common weapon throughout the Texian forces was probably the US musket pattern 1816, Type III, made between 1831 and 1844, and official issue to Republic of Texas troops from 1839. A conventional flintlock fitted with external barrel bands in the French manner, it had an unusual detachable brass priming pan.

D1: Sam Houston

This figure depicts Houston (1793–1863) in a costume which might have been worn by any Texian officer: civilian dress with the addition of a sash (not an official badge of rank), and a sabre and belt of US pattern. Houston's dress during the war was described by witnesses: Zuber noted him as '. . . a large, plainly dressed man riding a large, stout, clumsy-looking grey horse. . . . He wore plain coarse jeans, a white wool hat, and mud boots . . . notwithstanding his coarse attire, I thought that he was the noblest-looking man that I had ever seen.' J. H. Kuykendall noted Houston in the San Jacinto campaign wearing a 'black cloth dress coat' which was both threadbare and wet, someone having stolen his only blanket. During the campaign Houston often wore moccasins, as his boots were beginning to crack. Among his meagre equipment were saddlebags holding ears of raw corn to eat; a vial of mixed ammoniacal spirits and shavings of deer horn (a patent medicine to avert colds, which he sniffed so regularly that it gave rise to an erroneous rumour that he might be addicted to opium); and copies of *Gulliver's Travels* and (more appropriately) *Caesar's War Commentaries*, which he read far into the night, perhaps to gain inspiration for the coming battle.

Cannon found at La Bahía, probably used by Fannin's command, and now positioned near the memorial at the site of their grave. (Kevin R. Young)

D2: Texian cavalry scout

This figure wears typical frontier costume, representing Houston's trusted scout or 'spy', Erastus 'Deaf' Smith. This noted scout was married to a Mexican, and so versed in their language and customs that he could easily pass as Mexican. He had no interest in the war until Cós's men drove him away from San Antonio: he told Austin, 'I didn't want any part in this war . . . but since they have used me so treacherously, I now offer you my services . . . as a guide or spy.' It was a costly mistake by Cós's men as Smith, despite defective hearing, was one of the Texian army's greatest assets in intelligence gathering. In addition to the common 'round hat' and buckskin jacket, he wears Indian-style leather leggings which covered the upper part of the foot.

D3: Volunteer standard bearer with the 'San Jacinto Battle Flag'

This figure wears typical civilian costume, with the addition of the full US Army equipment (cartridge box, bayonet belt, musket and canteen) with which many Texians were equipped at San Jacinto. The flag is that now known as the 'San Jacinto Battle Flag', the only known colour carried by the Texians at the battle. It was made by the ladies of Newport, Kentucky, before Sidney Sherman's volunteer company left for Texas in late 1835, and showed an allegorical figure of Liberty bearing a sabre with the motto LIBERTY OR DEATH. The flag still exists in a worn and yellowed condition; it is shown in one (non-contemporary) painting as light blue in colour. Attached to the top of the staff was a lady's long, white kid glove, presented to the company as a good luck mascot on the eve of their departure for Texas.

D4: Texian volunteer officer

This figure is based on the uniform reputedly worn by Lt.Col. Sidney Sherman at San Jacinto, which may have been 'restored', together with a straw hat of a type not uncommon in Texas. The frock coat has black facings, including wide lapels, and gold lace; a reconstruction by J. Hefter shows rank bars on the shoulders—which, though they feature in portraits of Texian commanders painted after the war, were probably not worn at the time. J. H. Kuykendall saw Sherman in the San Jacinto campaign wearing a blue 'round jacket' laced silver, and carrying a 'handsome dress sword', with 'a trim and military appearance'. Burleson he described wearing a simple blue homespun 'round jacket' and pantaloons, and armed only with a brace of pistols in his belt. Sherman, a manufacturer of cotton bagging in Kentucky, sold his business to equip the volunteer company of 52 men which he led to Texas; he commanded the 2nd Regt. of Infantry at San Jacinto. He was later responsible for building the first railway in Texas.

E1: Santa Anna, campaign uniform
E2: General of Brigade, full dress

Mexican staff uniform was redesigned in August 1831 but retained features of 1823 and 1827. The dark blue coatee had red collar, cuffs, lining and piping, with horizontal pockets with three gilt buttons. One-inch gold embroidery was worn on the cuffs, collar and lapels, consisting of palm, laurel and olive leaves intertwined, but following no specific design, some examples being comparatively plain while others included flowers and scrolls. The gold lace epaulettes had heavy bullion fringes, and bore raised foliate designs on the strap, and a silver eagle. Two ranks existed: generals of division had a

'Maned' (rather than crested) version of the Mexican cavalry helmet. Black leather peak and skull with metal plate, comb and peak-edging; black horsehair mane. Plume at left side, and pompon at front of crest, in the Mexican colours of red, white and green.

'Dress' version of the hat of the Mexican Presidial companies (see Plate H3): black with white band, tricolour plume and cockade, white (or silver) cords. Rarely seen on the frontier.

double row of cuff embroidery, and wore a sky-blue sash with bullion tassels and a double row of embroidery on the knots; generals of brigade had single bands of embroidery on cuffs and sash knot, and green sashes with a single knot. White trousers were worn for full dress, and blue or grey for service. The bicorn hat had a tricolour cockade, gold lace edging, and often white 'feathering' and a tricolour panache. When not on duty generals were allowed to wear overcoats or frock coats, but always with the respective sash; those holding regimental commands were permitted to wear the uniform of their unit, but with general's epaulettes, sash and cuff embroidery.

Santa Anna is illustrated here wearing undress uniform, taken from Paris's painting of the Battle of Tampico (1829, but painted in 1836), though a Hefter reconstruction shows this uniform with scarlet facings. Though his frock coat is plain, as a general rule he delighted in wearing the most garishly ornamented of uniforms.

E3: Staff officer, Commandancies of Fortified Places, full dress

'Commandancies of Fortified Places' were created in 1835, each with a staff of a lieutenant-colonel, 12 officers, four NCOs and nine privates. Commandants of these wore regimental uniform when serving with their unit; at other times the staff uniform comprised a coatee of 'somewhat bright blue' with collar, lapels and cuffs of a darker shade, buttonholes trimmed with five-strand gold lace, a broad gold band around collar and cuffs leaving only one-third of the facing exposed, red piping, gilt buttons, and gold eagle turnback badges; blue overalls with a gold stripe, or plain white; unlaced blue lapels and trousers for service dress. Blue saddle cloth edged gold, gold tassels at the corners, fur-covered holster caps, and black harness and saddlery with silvered fittings.

E4: Captain, Reserve Cavalry

Taken in part from Paris's *The Battle of Tampico*, the officer illustrated wears Reserve Cavalry uniform (the colours of the regulars reversed: green faced red, though the Paris version shows green facings), with captain's epaulettes. The collar shown by Paris bears an embroidered silver foliate spray. The helmet has white metal fittings (also shown by some sources for the regulars, though the regulations

stated brass); and the straight-bladed sabre appears to resemble the Spanish 1825 pattern.

F1: Sergeant, Regular Cavalry

This figure wears the Mexican cavalry uniform, with a crested helmet. Cavalry weapons included a sabre suspended on a waistbelt and slings, pistol, and carbine, the latter carried in a saddle boot but with a slide attachment for suspension from the shoulder belt. Some cavalry carried muskets somewhat shorter than those of the infantry, with bayonets. The lance was nine feet long, with a three- or four-sided blade $8\frac{1}{4}$ inches long, attached to the shaft by two three-foot iron straps to prevent the head from being lopped off, and an iron cross-bar to prevent over-penetration; the swallow-tailed pennon was officially a foot long, but is often shown larger.

F2: Trooper, Light Cavalry

The regular cavalry converted to light troops in 1835 wore blue coatees with white metal buttons, similar colouring to that of the light infantry. The helmet worn by the man illustrated differs from the crested pattern of E4 and F1 in that it has a horsehair mane instead of a crest; both varieties were probably in use in 1835–36 and (though obsolete) the maned type remained in service as late

The walls and compound of Presidio La Bahía, as they might have appeared in 1836. The tower of the chapel can be seen left; in the right background is a bastion topped by a *guerite* or sentry box. The existence of 'living history' groups wearing authentic reproductions of the costume of the War of Independence is further testimony to the hold upon the Texan consciousness which the Alamo period still exerts. (Kevin R. Young)

as the US-Mexican War. In addition to these headdresses, light cavalry also used a fur busby or a shako with cords and chin scales.

F3: Sapper, Regular Cavalry

The figure illustrated, from Paris's *The Battle of Tampico*, wears the fur cap which traditionally distinguished sappers and farriers, with the ordinary cavalry uniform. Shabraques of the regular cavalry were green with white lace and white tassels at the ends; the lining was sailcloth or coarse brown linen. The green valises had red or green ends trimmed white, or green trimmed red, sometimes bearing the old regimental numbers. The wooden-framed saddle had iron stirrups (with a leather tube attached to the right stirrup, to support the lance butt) and leather holsters; the carbine was carried in a cylindrical leather boot at the right, muzzle down, or with the butt in a boot with a sling attached to the front of the saddle. The valise carried spare clothing, repair- and cleaning-kits; also carried was a sailcloth or coarse brown linen grain bag, an 18 inch-wide canvas sack containing apron and sponge, spare horseshoes in a saddle pocket, a blanket and cloak or overcoat beneath the valise, and a fatigue jacket and raincoat under the saddle roll.

G1: Corporal, Tres Villas Battalion

This corporal of the Tres Villas Bn. of Active Militia wears the single-breasted 1833-pattern jacket with rank bar on the sleeve, and the identification letters 'BTV' on the collar, though evidence for the use of this feature is inconclusive. The shako has no cords, in accordance with 1833 regulations, and the red plume worn by fusiliers. The shoulder belts support the cartridge box and bayonet; and a French-style sabre. Some sources show no belt plates. Though Militia uniforms were little different from those of the 'permanent' battalions, some units may not have had chin scales, only plain leather chinstraps. Though the Tres Villas possessed both dress and fatigue uniforms, they had no greatcoats, and suffered grievously from cold.

G2: 1st Sergeant, Matamoros Battalion

Based on a reconstruction by Joseph Hefter, this figure wears the 1832 coatee with plastron-style lapels. Though the shako has the green pompon of the chasseur company, the coatee does not have the *sardineta* lace of the 'preference' companies, this lace seemingly being applied in a somewhat irregular manner: his cuffs would resemble those of G1. The shako plate depicted is a more elaborate pattern than the oval variety; and the collar bears the 'BM' identification. The medium blue trousers with scarlet welts (a lighter shade than the 'dark blue' of the regulations) were an alternative to the white; it was apparently common practice to tie a rawhide thong below the knee. A reconstruction by Hefter (doyen of Mexican uniform historians) of the chasseurs of the Aldama Bn. shows green shako cords and lace, green pompon, facings and epaulettes.

G3: Grenadier, Infantry

This figure wears the 1833 jacket with the old collar numerals, and *sardineta* lace on the cuffs. The shako bears the grenade plate and red pompon of the grenadiers, and red braided cords and raquettes as specified in 1832 and 1835 but not in 1833; the

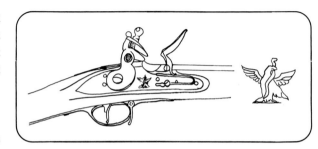

Lock of a Mexican 'Brown Bess' musket. The Mexican device of an eagle with a snake in its beak, stamped upon the lock-plate, is conclusive proof of the use of at least one version of 'Brown Bess' by the Mexican army at this period: an India Pattern with the reinforced cock introduced in 1809. In 1833 the British Ordnance still held some 440,000 India Pattern arms, 18 years after manufacture had ceased, so the sale of these over-stocks was an excellent opportunity for the Mexican government to obtain sturdy and effective firearms. The lock stamping is enlarged at the right.

grenade badge was also displayed on the flap of the cartridge box. The trousers are worn with the bottoms rolled up, apparently a common practice, and peasant-style sandals replace the boots. Like the other figures in this plate, the grenadier is armed with a British 'Brown Bess' musket.

G4: Fusilier, Infantry

This figure is based in part upon Paris, showing a rare rear view of Mexican infantry uniform, including vertical scarlet piping on the pocket flaps, and dark blue three-pointed shoulder straps piped scarlet in place of the fringeless epaulettes. (Some of the figures in this source have no piping to their scarlet facings.) Equipment consists of a hide knapsack with white straps, with a blanket or greatcoat rolled on top and secured by white strapping, and a bayonet carried on the belt over the right shoulder instead of on the cartridge box belt, with no sabre. The shako, based in part on Paris, is a variety featuring a coloured lace lower band instead of upper, with the yellow cords of fusilier companies, and a plume in the national red, white and green.

H1: Officer, Infantry, full dress

While Mexican infantry officers wore uniforms styled upon those of the rank and file, of finer quality and with epaulettes of rank, the figure illustrated (based in part upon an extant garment) wears a uniform having some similarity to the staff pattern, including foliate embroidery and a wide plastron front. The grey breeches and riding boots are campaign items, as is the plain sword belt. The shako plate is a variation on the oval pattern.

H2: Light Infantryman, campaign dress
This figure wears the uniform of those units designated light infantry in 1835: dark blue frock coat with red piping and yellow buttons, grey trousers, and a light, plain shako ornamented only with a pompon and a shield including the unit number or initials (though bugle-horn badges have been excavated, suggesting the use of this device by chasseurs and light infantry). He is armed with a British Baker rifle and its distinctive sword bayonet; such weapons were apparently reserved for chasseur companies and light infantry, but are unlikely to have been universal in such units. The scale of their use is hard to determine from Mexican sources couched in very general terms.

H3: Lancer, Presidial companies, campaign dress
Recalling the dress of the Spanish colonial gendarmerie or 'leather dragoons' from which the companies evolved, this figure shows the likely dress of the Presidial troops. The hat was basically a civilian style with turned-up brim and white decorations, tricolour cockade and plume. The blue coat had red facings, and though the 1821 regulations specified that a unit number be embroidered on the collar, initial letters of the province or *presidio* name seem to have been used. For garrison duty blue overalls with red stripe and black leather reinforcement were worn; but for field service, blue or grey loose-fitting overalls with red stripes, with protective buckskin gaiters worn under the overalls. When on service the hats were usually undecorated and worn with brim lowered; and the quilted leather sleeveless jerkin of earlier days may have been retained (at least in California) as late as 1846. The *presidio* name was often stitched on the shoulder belt. Arms comprised a sabre, carbine and lance. Matériel was often in short supply as in California in 1821 when the governor reported his men 'going about their duties entirely naked'.

H4: Artilleryman
Mexican artillery wore infantry-style uniform, with red collars bearing a yellow grenade, blue cuffs with red flaps, and red turnbacks; equipment seems to have included a short sabre, though Gen. Bravo

Memorial erected at the Fannin grave site to commemorate those executed at La Bahía (Goliad). (Kevin R. Young)

reported in 1836 that he had mounted artillery in Texas armed with sabres in steel scabbards and English *terceroles* (carbines). Mexican artillery was not in the best of condition: the horse artillery brigade had been suspended in November 1833 as its guns were in such a bad state. Artillery carriages had been painted light blue in the early years of the century, but may have been simply oiled at this period. The *Zapadores* battalion was uniformed similarly to the artillery, but with black facings and dark red piping, with red shako lace and a red tufted pompon resembling a bursting grenade. A reconstruction by Hefter of the uniform of Lt.Col. Agustin Amat of the *Zapadores* is in this style, but with deep red or crimson facings.

Sources
Histories and memoirs of the Texan War are legion; listed below are some important works and some of the most accessible for further reading:

J. J. Gaddy, *Texas in Revolt* (Ft Collins, Colo., 1973)

W. Lord, *A Time to Stand* (London, 1962) [Good modern study of the Alamo].

D. Nevin, *The Texans* (Time-Life, Alexandria, Va., 1975)

E. de la Peña, *With Santa Anna in Texas* (Texas A & M Univ. Press, 1975)

F. X. Tolbert, *Day of San Jacinto* (Austin & NY, 1959) [Modern study of the battle]; Texas State Hist. Assn. Quarterly, Vol. IV No. 4 (Austin, Tx., 1901) [This contains many eye-witness accounts].

Important works on the Mexican army and its costume are:

J. Hefter, *The Mexican Soldier* (Mexico City, 1958)
J. Hefter, *Cronica del Traje Militar en Mexico* (Mexico City, 1968)

Notes sur les planches en couleur

A1, 2, 3 Un mélange typique de vêtements de chasse, de vêtements de travail et de tenue civile 'achetée en magasin' de coupe plus conventionnelle. Les armes appartenaient généralement au soldat, et elles comprenaient le fusil 'Kentucky', long et précis; divers mousquets; et même des fusils de chasse à petit plomb. L'illustration présente aussi le canon de Gonzales, arme improvisée plus importante comme symbole de défi que comme pièce d'artillerie sérieuse!

B1 Travis porte un habit à queue et un chapeau rond typiques des années 1830; il avait commandé un uniforme mais celui-ci n'est arrivé qu'après sa mort. **B2** Crockett porte sa célèbre coiffe en raton laveur et une blouse de chasse sur des vêtements civils ordinaires; le fusil est sa vieille arme de chasse, 'Betsy'. **B3** Bowie, immortalisé par son fameux couteau, était plus célèbre comme bagarreur que comme soldat. En dépit de sa réputation de férocité en état d'ivresse, c'était en fait un homme courtois et calme.

C1 Les 'Red Rovers', provenant de la région de Courtland, Alabama, portaient cet uniforme bien attesté; la tenue complète comportait une veste et une coiffe en velours rouge, une ceinture en étoffe bleue et des pantalons blancs. L'*Alabama State Arsenal* fournissait un équipement personnel et des armes du type du gouvernement des Etats-Unis. **C2** Compagnie de volontaires bien équipée, qui ressemblait aux compagnies régulières; cet homme porte en fait une casquette 1825 des Etats-Unis. **C3** Un des nombreux déserteurs de l'armée des Etats-Unis ici, de l'artillerie qui se rendirent au sud pour aider le Texas. La casquette est du modèle pliant 1833 en cuir.

D1 La tenue civile de Houston, portée avec une ceinture en étoffe et une ceinture à sabre est sans doute typique pour tout officier texan de l'époque. Houston connaissait bien les indiens cherokee et portait souvent des mocassins. **D2** Portant une tenue de 'frontière' typique, ce personnage représente le fameux éclaireur Erastus Smith (Smith 'le Sourd'). **D3** En tenue civile typique avec un équipement de l'armée des Etats-Unis, ce texan porte le drapeau de la compagnie de Sidney Sherman, porté à la bataille de San Jacinto. **D4** Illustration basée sur un uniforme qui a paru-il-été porté par Lt.Col. Sherman à San Jacinto, avec addition d'un chapeau en paille typique.

E1 Santa Anna, portant la tenue de service une source montre cependant cette tenue avec des parements écarlates. **E2** L'uniforme de grande tenue des généraux de brigade comportait une bande de broderies aux manchettes et une ceinture en étoffe verte; les généraux de division portaient deux bandes de broderies et des ceintures en étoffe bleu ciel. L'uniforme était le modèle 1831 mais il conservait les caractéristiques des tenues précédentes de 1823 et 1827. **E3** Les officiers détachés auprès de ces organisations de garnison portaient l'uniforme du régiment lorsqu'ils étaient dans leurs unités et le reste du temps cet uniforme bleu vif aux parements d'un bleu plus foncé et aux nombreuses passementeries d'or. **E4** Les couleurs de la Cavalerie Régulière étaient inversées pour les Réserves vert avec parements rouges; notez casque avec pièces en métal blanc, et épaulettes de capitaine.

F1 Uniforme réglementaire et casque à crête; une carabine à la grenadière, un pistolet et un sabre étaient portés, et certaines unités avaient des lances. Des mousquets d'infanterie raccourcis, avec baïonnettes, étaient distribués au lieu de carabines dans certains cas. **F2** La Cavalerie Régulière transformée en Cavalerie Légère en 1835 portait une veste bleue avec des boutons en métal blanc. La coiffe pouvait être un casque à crête voir F1; ou de ce type, avec crins de cheval; un 'kolpack' de fourrure; ou un shako avec cordelettes et mentonnière. **F3** Etabli, comme la plupart de ces personnages, d'après le tableau 'The Battle of Tampico' de Paris, peint en 1836. Les caractéristiques du sapeur sont typiques de la plupart des armées de l'époque.

G1 Sous-officier d'une unité de milice active, avec veste de 1833 portant un galon de grade sur la manche et les premières lettres de l'unité ('BTV') sur le col. La plume rouge dénote une compagnie de fusiliers. **G2** D'après une reconstruction de Joseph Hefter: en dépit du pompon vert de la compagnie des chasseurs sur le shako, ce sous-officier n'a pas les broderies de manchette de la compagnie d'élite, qui semblaient souvent manquer. La veste est du type 1832, avec plastron. **G3** Notez la veste de 1833, avec numéro d'unité anachronique sur le col; accessoires de shako de couleur rouge de la compagnie de grenadiers et broderies de compagnie d'élite aux manchettes. **G4** Paris montre cette vue arrière; les cordelettes jaunes et la plume tricolore dénotent un fusilier; notez la bande inférieure de couleur du shako, qui est une variation connue. Tous ces hommes portent les mousquets britanniques 'Brown Bess'.

H1 Illustration partiellement établie sur une tunique parvenue jusqu'à nous qui possède quelques caractéristiques 'état-major' de haute qualité; les pantalons gris et les bottes de cavalerie étaient portés en campagne. **H2** La tenue réglementaire 1835 pour l'Infanterie Légère est illustrée ici; le fusil britannique 'Baker' était distribué dans une certaine mesure aux troupes légères. **H3** Reconstitution de l'uniforme probable de ces compagnies, ayant pour origine la vieille gendarmerie coloniale espagnole dont les membres étaient appelés 'dragons de cuir' du fait de leurs gilets et jambières de protection en cuir (qui ont peut-être survécu jusque dans les années 1830 dans certains cas). **H4** Uniforme essentiellement du style cavalerie, avec détails d'insigne et de parement d'artillerie. Les *Zapadores* portaient un uniforme similaire avec parements noirs, des passepoils rouges et des garnitures de shako rouges.

Farbtafeln

A1, 2, 3 Eine typische Auswahl von Jagd- und Arbeitsbekleidung und formelleren, 'von der Stange' gekauften zivilen Stücken. Waffen sind gewöhnlich im Privatbesitz, darunter das lange und sehr präzise 'Kentucky'-Gewehr, verschiedene Musketen und sogar Vogelschrotflinten. Abgebildet ist ausserdem die 'Kanone von Gonzales', eine improvisierte Waffe, weniger ein Beispiel für ernsthafte Artillerie als ein Symbol des Widerstands.

B1 Travis trägt den typischen zivilen Frack und 'runden Hut' der 1830er Jahre: Die von ihm bestellte Uniform kam erst nach seinem Tod an. **B2** Crockett trägt seine berühmte Washbärkappe und eine Jägerjacke über der konventionellen zivilen Kleidung; das Gewehr ist sein altes Jagdgewehr 'Betsey'. **B3** Der durch sein berühmtes Messer unsterbliche Bowie war als Randalierer bekannter denn als Soldat. Trotz seines schlechten Rufs als Trunkenbold war er ein höflicher, zurückhaltender Mann.

C1 Die 'Red Rovers' aus Courtland (Alabama) trugen diese vielfach bezeugte Uniform; die volle Ausführung schloss eine Kappe aus rotem Samt und eine Jacke, Schärpe und weisse Hosen ein. Das *Alabama State Arsenal* vertrieb Waffen und persönliche Ausrüstungsgegenstände nach dem Muster der US-Regierung. **C2** Eine gut ausgestattete Freiwilligenkompanie, ähnlich den regulären Truppen; dieser Mann trägt eine amerikanische Feldmütze von 1825. **C3** Einer von vielen Deserteuren der *US Army*, in diesem Fall von der Artillerie, der zur Unterstützung von Texas in den Süden ging. Die Feldmütze ist die lederne Faltausführung von 1833.

D1 Houstons mit Schärpe und Säbelgürtel getragene zivile Uniform ist vielleicht typisch für texanische Offiziere dieser Epoche. Houston war mit der Cherokee-Indianern vertraut und trug häufig Mokkassins. **D2** Diese Figur in typischer Grenzland-Bekleidung ist der bekannte Scout Erastus Smith 'Der taube Smith'. **D3** Dieser Texaner in typischer Zivilbekleidung mit US Army-Ausrüstung trägt die Flagge der Sydney Sherman Kompanie, die bei der Schlacht von San Jacinto getragen wurde. **D4** Nach einer angeblich von Lt.Col. Sherman in San Jacinto getragenen Uniform, mit zusätzlichem typischem Strohhut.

E1 Santa Anna mit 'Ausziehuniform' eine andere Quelle zeigt scharlachfarbene Aufschläge. **E2** Die volle Ausgehuniform eines Brigadegenerals hatte nun einen bestickten Streifen an den Manschetten und eine grüne Schärpe; Divisionsgenerale trugen zwei Streifen und hellblaue Schärpen. Die Uniform war ein Modell aus dem Jahr 1831 mit Kennzeichen der Regeln von 1823 und 1827. **E3** Die diesen Garrisonsorganisationen zugeordneten Offiziere trugen Regimentsuniformen bei ihren Einheiten, sonst diese hellblaue Uniform mit dunkelblauem Aufsatz und reichem Goldbesatz. **E4** Die Farben für die Regulären wurden für die Freiwilligen umgekehrt grün mit rot besetzt; ein Helm mit weissem Metallbesatz und Epauletten für den Hauptmann sind ebenfalls abgebildet.

F1 Reguläre Uniform und Federhelm; umgehängter Karabiner, Pistole und Säbel; einige Einheiten hatten auch Lanzen. Verkürzte Infanteriemusketen mit Bajonetten wurden in einigen Fällen anstelle der Karabiner ausgegeben. **F2** Die 1835 auf leichte Kavallerie umgestellten Einheiten trugen blaue Jacken und silbernes 'Metall'. Die Kopfbedeckung war möglicherweise ein geschmückter Helm (siehe F1) oder dieser Typ mit Rosshaarmähne, ein Pelz-Kolpak, oder ein Tschako mit Schnüren und Kinnhalter. **F3** Wie die meisten dieser Figurinen auf Paris' Gemälde 'The Battle of Tampico' aus dem Jahre 1836 basierend. Die Sappeur-Kennzeichen sind typisch für die meisten Armeen dieser Zeit.

G1 Unteroffizier einer aktiven Milizeinheit mit einer Jacke von 1835 und Rangabzeichen auf dem Ärmel sowie den Anfangsbuchstaben der Einheit ('BTV') am Kragen. Die rote Federbusch verweist auf eine Füsilierkompanie. **G2** Nach einer Rekonstruktion von Joseph Hefter; trotz des grünen Pompon der Chasseur-Kompanie hat dieser Unteroffizier nicht den Manschettenbesatz der 'Präferenzkompanie', der anscheinend häufig fehlte. Die Jacke ist im Stil von 1832 mit Plastron. **G3** Man beachte die Jacke von 1835 mit überholter Einheitsnummer am Kragen, rote Tschakoteile der Grenadierkompanie und die korrekte Manschettenbesatz der 'Präferenzkompanie'. **G4** Paris bietet diese Rückansicht; die gelben Schnüre und der dreifarbige Federbusch verweisen auf einen Füsilier; man beachte das farbige untere Tschakoband, eine bekannte Variante. Alle diese Männer tragen britische 'Brown Bess' Musketen.

H1 Teilweise auf einem erhalten gebliebenen Mantel basierend, mit einigen bedeutenden Kennzeichen; die grauen Gamaschen und Reitstiefel wurden bei Feldzügen getragen. **H2** Hier sind die Bestimmungen für die leichte Infanterie aus dem Jahre 1835 illustriert; das britische Baker-Gewehr wurde in gewissen Mengen an leichte Truppen ausgegeben. **H3** Wahrscheinliche Rekonstruktion der Uniform dieser Kompanien, die auf den altspanischen Knlonialsergeante ('Lederdragoner' wegen der Schutzgilets aus Ochsenhaut und den in manchen Fällen vielleicht bis in die 1830er Jahre erhalten gebliebenen Beinschützern beruhen. **H4** Uniform grundsätzlich im Infanteristil, mit Artilleriebesatz und Abzeichendetails. Die *Zapadores* trugen ähnliche Bekleidung mit schwarzem Besatz, roten Kordeln und roten Tschakoteilen.